AMISH & MENNONITE

Photo : Doyle Yoder

BEAUTIFUL QUILTS

AMISH
&
MENNONITE

making classic quilts and modern variations

KATHARINE GUERRIER

illustrations by

PENNY BROWN

Museum Quilts

Published by Museum Quilts (UK) Inc.
254-258 Goswell Road, London EC1V 7EB

The author has endeavoured to ensure that all project instructions are accurate. However, due to
variations in readers' individual skill and materials available, neither the author nor the publisher can accept
responsibility for damages or losses resulting from the instructions herein. All instructions should be studied
and clearly understood before beginning any project.

Editors: Ljiljana Baird and Annlee Landman
Designers: Bet Ayer and Opas Chantkam

A CIP catalogue record for this book is available from the British Library

ISBN: 1-897954-56-5

Printed and bound in France by Partenaires

CONTENTS

Introduction 6

Bow-Tie

Mennonite Bow-Tie 8

Calico Bow-Ties 12

Snowballs 15

Kaleidoscope 17

Bear's Paw

Amish Bear's Paw 18

Miniature Bear's Paw 23

Straight Set Bear's Paw 25

Optical Bear's Paw 27

Baskets

Mennonite Baskets 28

Cake Stand 32

Autumn Baskets 35

Cross and Crown 37

Diamond in a Square

Amish Diamond in a Square 38

Spools 42

Criss-Cross Diamonds 45

Pyramids 49

Log Cabin

Mennonite Straight Furrows 50

Courthouse Steps 55

Miniature Barn Raising 58

Black-eyed Sue 61

Bars

Mennonite Joseph's Coat 62

Chinese Coins Crib Quilt 66

Diamond Bars 68

Climbing Roses 71

Sunshine and Shadow

Amish Sunshine and Shadow 72

Philadelphia Pavement 76

Mosaic Tiles 78

Railroad Crossing 81

Irish Chain

Mennonite Double Irish Chain 82

Single Irish Chain 86

Triple Irish Chain 89

Pumpkin Patch 93

Nine-Patch

Amish Nine-Patch 94

Scrap Nine-Patch 98

Double Nine-Patch 101

Mandarin Chequerboard 104

Basic Techniques 105

Piecing Templates 116

Quilting Templates 118

Index 128

INTRODUCTION

Known as 'The Plain People', the Amish and Mennonite communities today are descended from the Anabaptists, the radical Protestant reformists who fled Europe in the mid-eighteenth century to avoid religious persecution. The Amish and the more conservative congregations of the Mennonite Church remain as insular groups rejecting modern technology such as motorised transport, telephones and electricity in favour of a simple, unadorned way of life which has remained virtually unchanged for 300 years. This identifies them to outsiders as separate groups while giving them a cohesive identity. Other lifestyles are rejected and all outsiders labelled as 'The English'.

Communities are governed by the 'Ordung', a code of traditions and customs drawn from the Bible which influences all aspects of daily life. This is largely orally transmitted and provides spiritual, social and economic guidelines by which each community lives. Different church districts have varying degrees of conservatism.

The Quilts

Few written records exist from Amish and Mennonite communities; a tradition of passing on the values and culture orally from one generation to the next means that little is known of the design origins of Amish quilts. Interaction with neighbouring communities seems to have had some influence and by the 1860s quiltmaking among the Amish and Mennonite was beginning to be an established activity. Taking the idea of the pieced quilt from 'The English', they began to develop their own unique style which, while satisfying a practical need, was tempered by the limitations imposed by religious beliefs.

Their quilts, in particular the antique woollen ones which survive today, are noted for their graphic simplicity. Powerful yet simple geometric designs, which frequently use intense colours have provoked parallels to be drawn between the visual impact of these quilts and contemporary abstract art movements. Designs such as Centre Diamond, Bars and Sunshine and Shadow are typical. These are characterised by sombre colours enlivened by small accents of pure, bright pinks, reds and greens giving the effect of 'sparkle' in these deceptively simple designs.

The pieced block was often used to interpret and depict familiar everyday objects with much ingenuity. Baskets, Bear's Paw, Bow-Tie and Log Cabin are examples presented in this collection of quilts and there are many others. Family traditions often dictated the selection of the quilt design to be made. Often the older women of the family would do the piecing, and most quilts made after 1860 were pieced by treadle machine. On completion of the quilt top, the three layers of the quilt were assembled. The backing, often printed with a small check or tiny flower sprigs, and the middle layer or filler were added, making the fabric 'sandwich' which forms the quilt. Original Amish and Mennonite quilts had a wool wadding which required close quilting stitches to hold it in place and prevent all the filling from shifting. The quilting stitches were both functional and decorative, and great pride was taken in the small, even stitches which added surface texture to the quilt top. Motifs stitched onto Amish quilts included flower baskets, stars and tulips, and border designs such as cables and running feather designs, as well as geometric straight line grids, which were used as infill stitches.

Many of the activities necessary for survival required the involvement of the whole community. Barn-raising, harvesting and corn husking were co-operative efforts, and a quilting 'bee' or 'frolic' was no exception. Finished quilt tops, often pieced through the winter were set up with the filler and backing on the quilting frame and as many women as could fit around the edges stitched the three layers of the quilt together, often in just one day. Children of the family helped by keeping a supply of threaded needles ready for use; others helped by preparing food for the large gathering that

followed. These co-operative activities aimed at mutual aid combined with an important social occasion to reinforce the sense of community important to each member.

A study of old Amish and Mennonite quilts will reveal a legacy of strong designs and striking colours, each a testament to the ingenuity and creativity of its maker. The nine wonderful quilts which prompted this book can be seen at the Museum Quilts Gallery, in London. The vitality of each quilt inspired me to analyse its construction, and wonder about how it would look if I rearranged its components. By changing the fabric placement, or choosing a different colour scheme, by introducing sashing or removing borders, by turning the blocks on point a variety of new quilt designs have emerged.

There is great satisfaction to be had from designing, as well as making quilts, and I hope that this book will encourage all quilters to create a quilt of their own imagining.

Mennonite Bow-Tie

BOW-TIE

Despite the simplicity of the Bow-Tie block - composed of just five pieces - it is surprisingly versatile and can be used to create a number of different quilt designs. This is in part due to its diagonal nature; different effects can be created by organising the light and dark values and varying the sets.

In the first quilt presented here, the blocks are set together in groups of four, separated and framed by broad bands of pink sashing and punctuated by grey corner squares.

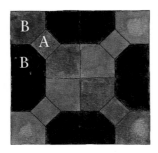

Skill level: Intermediate
Finished quilt: 75 x 75 in / 190.5 x 190.5 cm
Finished block: 9 x 9 in / 22.9 x 22.9 cm
Number of blocks: 25

MATERIALS

Black 1¹/₂ yards / metres
Assorted solids to total 2 yards / metres
     Each bow-tie block requires a scrap of black
     6 x 12 in / 15.2 x 30.5 cm and one scrap each of
     two colours 6 x 8 in / 15.2 x 20.3 cm
Pink fabric for sashing and borders 3 yards / metres
Grey fabric for posts 16 x 16 in / 40.6 x 40.6 cm
Wadding 80 x 80 in / 203.2 x 203.2 cm
Backing 4¹/₂ yards / metres
Binding ³/₄ yard / metre

CUTTING INSTRUCTIONS

Assorted plain fabrics
1. Trace and make templates A and B. Although it
is recommended that the block is hand-pieced, the
template has a seam allowance for those who wish
to machine-piece. If you are hand-piecing, use the
dotted line as a guide for tracing and add the seam
allowance as you cut out the fabric, as described in
the Techniques section.
2. For each block, use template B to cut four pieces
in each of two colours. Cut two pieces in each of
the same two colours using Template A.

Pink fabric
1. Cut two border strips, 9¹/₂ x 62 in / 24.1 x 157.5
cm, and two strips, 9¹/₂ x 79 in / 24.1 x 200.6 cm.
Excess length has been allowed for trimming to fit
when borders are attached.
2. Cut 40 strips, 3¹/₂ x 9¹/₂ in / 8.9 x 24.1 cm for
the sashing.

Grey fabric
1. Cut 16 squares, 3¹/₂ x 3¹/₂ in / 8.9 x 8.9 cm for
the corner posts which separate the sashing.

Binding fabric
1. Cut eight strips, 2¹/₂ in / 6.4 cm wide across the
full width of the fabric. Join together as required.

PIECING THE BLOCKS

1. Following the
piecing diagrams, place
piece A (knot) and
piece B (tie) right sides
together. Match mid-
point of the seam by
pinning a crease in both
pieces then stitching
the seam along marked
line and within seam
allowances.

2. Repeat with another
B piece.

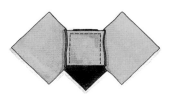

3. Sew the first background B piece to the knot along the corresponding side of the bow. Begin and end your seam on the sewing line without stitching into the seam allowance.

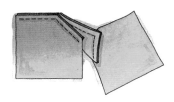

4. Pivot to align bow and background pieces and stitch side seams, working away from the centre.

5. Repeat for the other side seams.

6. Add the second background piece in the same way.

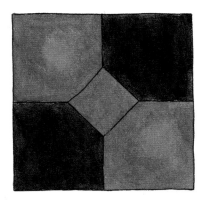

7. Press seams away from the centre.

8. Make four units for each block, referring to the picture for placement. When stitching the four units of the block together, arrange seam allowances at the edges so that they will butt with adjoining blocks to reduce bulk.

9. Make 24 more blocks.

PUTTING THE BLOCKS TOGETHER

1. Arrange the blocks in five horizontal rows of five blocks each, on a flat surface with the colours distributed as desired. Sew rows of blocks together with a sashing strip between each one. Press.
2. Stitch the remaining sashing strips together with a corner post between each strip.
3. Join the rows of blocks together connected by the long sashing strips, matching points.

ADDING THE BORDERS

1. Attach the two shorter border lengths to the top and bottom of the quilt.
2. Attach the two longer border lengths to the sides.

QUILTING AND FINISHING

1. Press the quilt carefully. Remove any loose threads.
2. Transfer the circular quilting design supplied to the borders. Straight line quilting has been used on the centre panel to complement the blocks by echoing the geometric shapes. This can be marked as you work with 1/4 in / 6 mm masking tape.
3. Assemble the quilt layers and baste in a grid.
4. Quilt, working from the centre outwards.
5. When quilting is complete, join the binding strips as necessary to make the appropriate lengths for the sides, top and bottom, and finish the edges with a folded, straight binding as directed in the Techniques section.

CALICO BOW-TIES

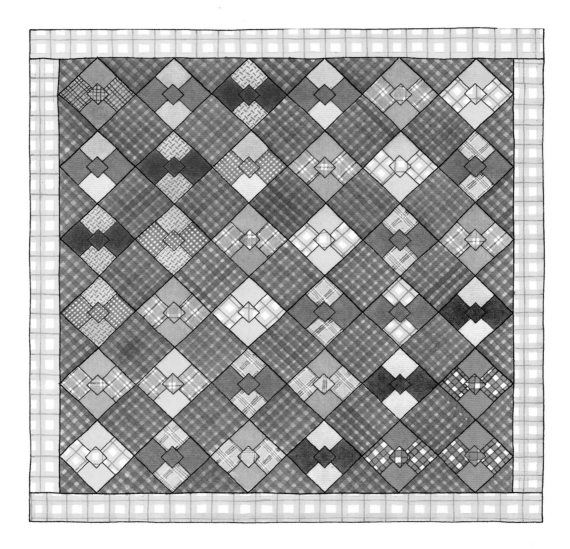

The representational aspect of the block is accentuated in this variation;
the 'knot' of the bow-tie is turned and set at a jaunty angle. The fabric
combination of plaids and small prints, gives the quilt a distinctly
nostalgic appeal reminiscent of the 1930s.

Skill level: Easy
Finished quilt: 51 x 51 in / 129.5 x 129.5 cm
Finished block: 6 x 6 in / 15.2 x 15.2 cm
Number of blocks: 36

MATERIALS

Blue plaid 1³/₄ yards / metres
Yellow plaid 1³/₄ yards / metres
Assorted scraps to total 1 yard / metre
   One block will need 1 piece 8 x 6 in / 20.3 x
   15.2 cm and 1 piece 8 x 4 in / 20.3 x 10.2 cm
Wadding 55 x 55 in / 139.7 x 139.7 cm.
Backing 1¹/₂ yards / metres
Binding ¹/₂ yard / metre

CUTTING INSTRUCTIONS

Yellow plaid fabric

1. Cut two strips 4¹/₂ x 54 in / 11.4 x 137.2 cm, and two strips 4¹/₂ x 63 in / 11.4 x 160 cm for the borders. Extra length has been allowed for trimming to fit once borders are attached.

Blue plaid fabric

1. Cut 25 setting squares, 6¹/₂ x 6¹/₂ in / 16.5 x 16.5 cm.
2. Cut five squares, 9³/₄ x 9³/₄ in / 24.8 x 24.8 cm. Cut across both diagonals to make 20 side triangles.
3. Cut two squares, 5¹/₄ x 5¹/₄ in / 13.3 x 13.3 cm. Cut diagonally in half to make four corner triangles.

Assorted scrap fabrics

The blocks can be cut out as you work. For each block you will need two different fabrics.

1. From one fabric scrap, cut two squares, 3¹/₂ x 3¹/₂ in / 8.9 x 8.9 cm, and one square 2 x 2 in / 5.1 x 5.1 cm for the bow-tie.
2. From another scrap, cut two squares, 3¹/₂ x 3¹/₂ in / 8.9 x 8.9 cm for the background.

PIECING THE BLOCKS

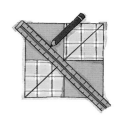

1. Piece the larger squares together into a four-patch. Draw diagonal line across the pieced block with a fabric marker or crease with an iron.

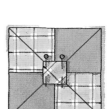

2. Turn a narrow hem ¹/₄ in / 6 mm all round the edges of the smaller square. Position it over the centre of the four-patch with the corners in line with the diagonal line. Stitch down over the centre of the four-patch by hand or machine.

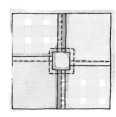

3. Turn the block over and clip away the centre of the four-patch behind the small square, ¹/₄ in / 6 mm in from the seam to eliminate excess bulk.

4. Make 35 more blocks, referring to the picture for ideas on fabric combinations.

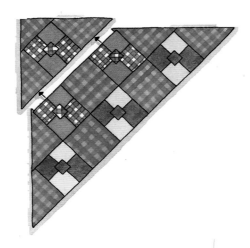

PUTTING THE BLOCKS TOGETHER

1. Alternate the pieced blocks with the blue plaid setting squares distributing colours as desired.
2. Place side or corner triangles at each end of the rows as appropriate.
3. Stitch the blocks together. Press seams towards the setting squares.
4. Stitch the diagonal rows of blocks together, taking care to match seams.

ADDING THE BORDERS

1. Add the two shorter borders to the sides of the centre panel, trimming the lengths of the borders even with the edges of the quilt to fit.
2. Add the two longer borders to the top and bottom of the quilt. Trim as before, and press.

QUILTING AND FINISHING

1. Give the quilt top a final press on the back and front and trim away any loose threads.
2. Mark the setting squares with a quilting design before layering, using your preferred method. Straight line quilting such as contour or grid designs can be marked as you work with $1/4$ in / 6 mm masking tape.
3. Assemble the three layers of the quilt and baste in a grid.
4. Quilt, working from the centre outwards.
5. When quilting is complete, finish the edges with a continuous separate binding as directed in the Techniques section.

SNOWBALLS

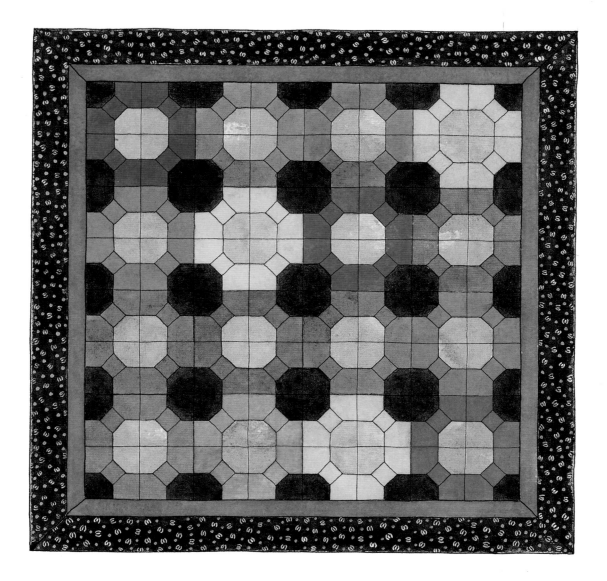

Pure, solid colours are used in this variation, one in which the
secondary design of the blocks emerges to form strong, dark octagons.

Skill level: Intermediate
Finished quilt: 48 x 48 in / 121.9 x 121.9 cm
Finished block: 9 x 9 in / 22.9 x 22.9 cm
Number of blocks: 16

MATERIALS

Pale grey ¹/₂ yard / metre

Black ³/₄ yard / metre

Assorted plain bright colours for a total of 1¹/₂ yards / metres

 Each block needs a scrap, 9 x 13 in / 22.9 x 33 cm

Blue for border ¹/₂ yard / metre

Black print for border and binding 1¹/₂ yards / metres

Wadding 52 x 52 in / 132 x 132 cm

Backing 3 yards / metres

CUTTING INSTRUCTIONS

Black print fabric

1. Cut four outer border strips, 4¹/₂ x 54 in / 11.4 x 137.2 cm. This allows a generous amount for the mitred corners.

Blue fabric

1. Cut four inner border strips, 2¹/₂ in / 6.4 cm wide across the width of the fabric to allow for the mitred corners.

Black fabric

1. Trace and make templates as directed for the 'Mennonite Bow-Ties' quilt.

2. Using template B, cut 64 pieces.

Pale grey fabric

1. Using template B, cut 64 pieces.

Assorted bright fabrics

1. From each scrap, cut four pieces using template A and eight pieces using template B.

PIECING THE BLOCKS

1. Piece the blocks in the same way as for the 'Mennonite Bow-Ties' referring to the picture for the correct placement of colours within the block.

2. Make 16 blocks.

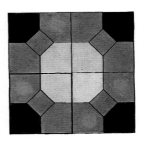

PUTTING THE BLOCKS TOGETHER

1. Arrange the blocks on a flat surface, positioning the different colours as desired.

2. Stitch the blocks together into sets of four, then eight and finally into a panel of 16. This will avoid having to sew all but one long seam.

3. Press well on the back and front and trim away any loose threads.

ADDING THE BORDERS

1. Stitch the inner blue borders to the centre panel, mitring the corners as directed in the Techniques section.

2. Repeat with the black print borders.

QUILTING AND FINISHING

1. Mark the areas created by the plain black and pale grey fabrics with a decorative circular motif if desired. Contour or grid quilting can be marked as you work with ¹/₄ in / 6 mm masking tape.

2. Assemble the quilt layers and baste in a grid.

3. Quilt, working from the centre outwards.

4. When quilting is complete, make continuous bias binding from the remaining black print and apply a folded bias binding with mitred corners, as directed in the Techniques section.

KALEIDOSCOPE

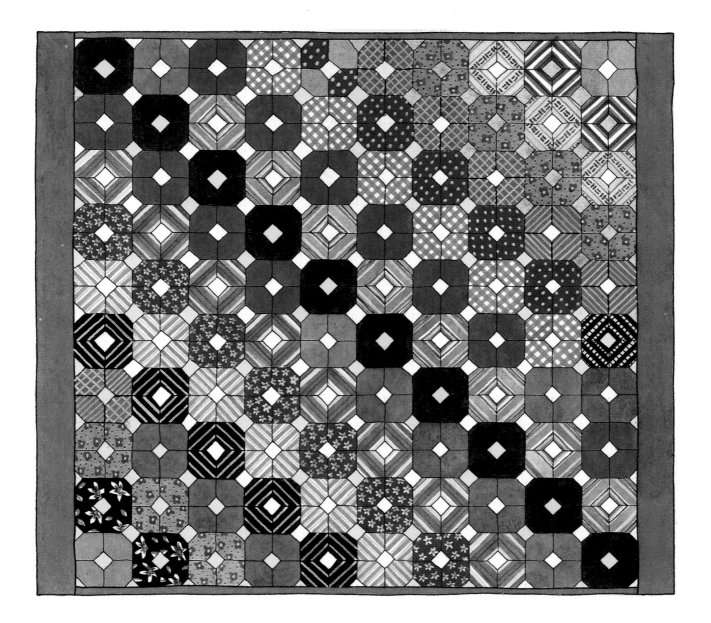

In this version of the Bow-Tie block, the extensive combination of fabrics gives the quilt a rich surface texture and a lively sense of movement. The blocks are set together in the same way as Snowballs but the visual differences between these two interpretations illustrate the diverse possibilities from one basic theme.

Amish Bear's Paw

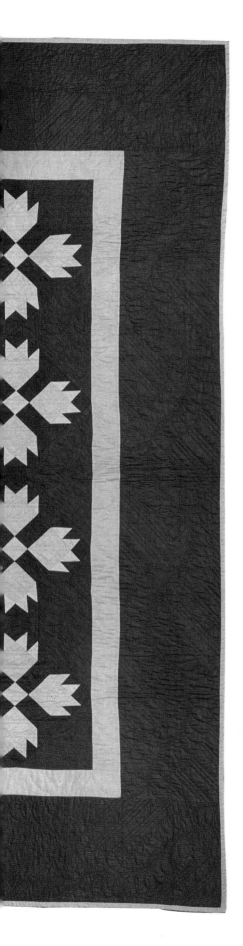

BEAR'S PAW

A navy and lilac combination provides a striking contrast for the first quilt in this set. The delicacy of the 'claw' motif is enhanced by setting the blocks on point, and each complete 'Bear's Paw' floats in a field of navy created by the setting squares. The proportions of the two borders complement this pleasing abstract composition.

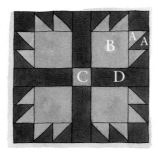

Skill level: Intermediate
Finished quilt: 73 x 83 in /185.4 x 210.8 cm
Finished block: 8³/4 x 8³/4 in / 22.2 x 22.2 cm
Number of blocks: 20

MATERIALS

Navy 3³/4 yards / metres
Lilac 2¹/2 yards / metres
Backing 5 yards / metres
Wadding 76 x 85 in / 193 x 215.9 cm

CUTTING INSTRUCTIONS

All the pieces can be cut without templates using the rotary cutting method. The half-square triangle units can be quick-pieced using the measurements and method described for block assembly. All measurements include ¹/4 in / 6 mm seam allowances. Generous border and binding lengths have been given to allow for trimming to fit as necessary.

Navy fabric
1. Cut two strips 10 x 85¹/2 in / 25.4 x 217.2 cm, and two strips 8³/4 x 57¹/2 in / 22.2 x 146.1 cm for the outer borders.
2. Cut three squares, 13⁵/8 x 13⁵/8 in / 34.5 x 34.5 cm. Then cut across both diagonals into four quarters to make 12 side triangles. Using one triangle as a template, cut two more side triangles making sure the straight grain of the fabric runs along the base of the triangle.
3. Cut two squares, 7¹/8 x 7¹/8 in / 18.1 x 18.1 cm in half diagonally to make four corner triangles.
4. Cut twelve setting squares, 9¹/4 x 9¹/4 in / 23.5 x 23.5 cm.
5. Cut 20 rectangles, 6 x 10 in / 15.2 x 25.4 cm for quick-piecing half-square A units.
6. Cut 80 C squares, 1³/4 x 1³/4 in / 4.4 x 4.4 cm.
7. Cut 80 D rectangles, 1³/4 x 4¹/4 in / 4.4 x 10.8 cm.

Lilac fabric
1. Cut two strips, 2¹/2 x 53¹/2 in / 6.4 x 135.9 cm, and two strips, 2¹/2 x 70 in / 6.4 x 17.8 cm for inner borders.
2. Cut eight strips, 2¹/2 in / 6.4 cm wide across the full width of the fabric for the binding.
3. Cut 20 rectangles, 6 x 10 in / 15.2 x 25.4 cm for quick-piecing half-square A units.
4. Cut 80 B squares, 3 x 3 in / 7.6 x 7.6 cm.
5. Cut 20 C squares, 1³/4 x 1³/4 in / 4.4 x 4.4 cm.

PIECING THE BLOCKS

1. To quick-piece the half-square A units, first assemble and press (with right sides facing) the navy and lilac rectangles into 20 sets. Using a sharp pencil, mark a rectangle 4¹/4 x 8¹/2 in / 10.8 x 21.6 cm in the middle of the lilac fabric. Mark a grid, 2¹/8 in / 5.4 cm inside the rectangle, and then draw diagonal line across the squares in one direction only.

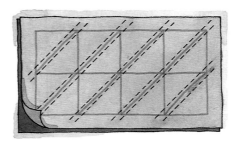

2. Sew ¹/4 in / 6 mm away from both sides of each diagonal pencil line.

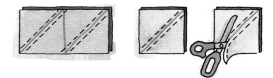

3. Cut along the horizontal and vertical grid line, then on each diagonal line. Unpick the few stitches which cross some of the corners and press the seams to the darker side. Each set of rectangles will make 16 A units.

4. Sew two A units together to make a pair. Repeat until you have sewn four pairs.

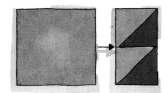

5. Sew a B square to the lilac edge of each A-A pair.

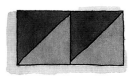

6. Sew the remaining A units together, reversing the orientation. Add a navy C square to the lilac edge.

7. Sew A/B units to A/C units to form four 'paws'.

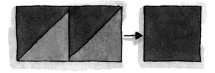

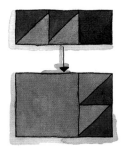

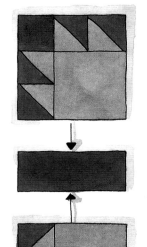

8. Make half of the block by sewing a D strip between two 'paw' units. Be sure to turn the bottom unit so that the 'claws' are on the outside edge.

9. Follow the same sequence for the other half of the block. Press towards the D strip.

10. Join the two remaining D pieces to opposite sides of a lilac C square to make the central dividing strip. Press towards the D strip.

11. To complete the block, sew the three components together being careful to match seams accurately at each junction.

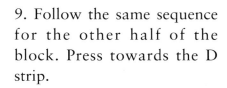

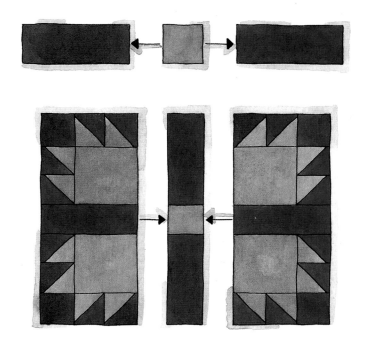

PUTTING THE BLOCKS TOGETHER

1. Refer to the quilt assembly diagram and arrange the pieced blocks alternately with the setting blocks. Place the side and corner triangles in the correct position.

2. Pin, then stitch the blocks together into diagonal rows. Press seams towards the setting squares.

3. Stitch the rows together in the correct order, taking care to match the seams.

ADDING THE BORDERS

1. Sew the short lilac borders to the sides of the quilt and press. Sew remaining lilac borders to the top and bottom. Press.

2. Sew the outer borders first to the sides, then to the top and bottom of the quilt, pressing in between steps.

QUILTING AND FINISHING

1. Give the quilt top a final press and tidy the back, trimming away any loose threads and seam allowances which may show through to the front of the quilt.

2. From the quilting patterns supplied, transfer a feather design to the borders and circular pie-plate design to the setting squares using your preferred method.

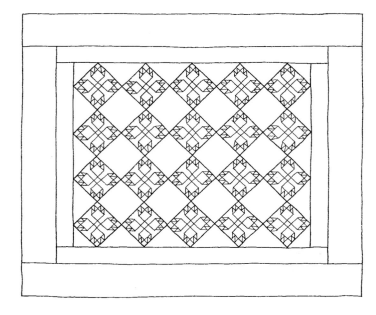

3. Cut the backing fabric into two equal lengths. Match selvedges, then sew a seam down one long side using a 1/2 in / 1.3 cm seam allowance. Press the seam to one side, then trim off selvedges. Press.

4. Assemble the quilt layers, and baste in a grid.

5. Quilt, working from the centre outwards.

6. Trim the backing and wadding even with the quilt top.

7. Sew binding strips together into four lengths 1/2 in / 1.3 cm longer than the sides of the quilt.

8. Apply the prepared binding strips to the raw edges of the quilt, following the instructions in the Techniques section.

MINIATURE BEAR'S PAW

In this variation the block is scaled down in size and more fabrics
have been added, giving the design a contemporary look.

Skill level: Intermediate / Advanced
Finished block: 5¹/4 x 5¹/4 in / 13.3 x 13.3 cm
Finished quilt: 29 x 36¹/2 in / 73.7 x 92.7 cm
Number of blocks: 20

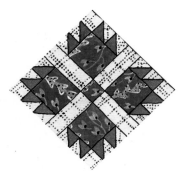

MATERIALS

Blue print 1/4 yard / metre
Red 1/4 yard / metre
Light background 3/4 yard / metre
Russet print 1/2 yard / metre
Backing 1 1/4 yards / metres
Low-loft wadding 33 x 40 in / 83.8 x 101.6 cm

CUTTING INSTRUCTIONS

Russet print

1. Cut 12 E setting squares, 5 3/4 x 5 3/4 in / 14.6 x 14.6 cm.

2. Cut four squares, 8 3/4 x 8 3/4 in / 22.2 x 22.2 cm. Cut each square twice on the diagonals to make a total of 16 side triangles. Although only 14 are required, this cutting method ensures that the straight grain of the fabric will run parallel with the sides of the quilt.

3. Cut two squares, 4 5/8 x 4 5/8 in / 11.7 x 11.7 cm. Cut each square diagonally in half to make four corner triangles.

Blue print

1. Cut two strips, 2 x 35 in / 5.1 x 88.9 cm and two strips, 2 x 43 in / 5.1 x 109.2 cm. Set the four strips aside for the binding.

2. Cut 80 B squares, 2 x 2 in / 5.1 x 5.1 cm and 20 C squares, 1 1/4 x 1 1/4 in / 3.2 x 3.2 cm for the pieced blocks.

Red fabric

1. Cut 20 rectangles, 5 x 8 in / 12.7 x 20.3 cm for quick-piecing the A half-square units.

Light background

1. Cut 20 rectangles, 5 x 8 in / 12.7 x 20.3 for quick-piecing the A half-square units.

2. Cut 80 C squares, 1 1/4 x 1 1/4 in / 3.2 x 3.2 cm and 80 D rectangles, 1 1/4 x 2 3/4 in / 3.2 x 7 cm for the pieced blocks.

PIECING THE BLOCKS

1. To make the half-square A units, follow the same instructions as for the larger quilt but draw a 1 5/8 in / 4.1 cm grid. Use a standard 1/4 in / 6 mm seam allowance as instructed, but trim the excess down to 1/8 in / 3 mm after sewing. This will reduce the bulk on the finished block. It is also important to press seams open, rather than towards the darker fabric.

2. Continue to piece 20 miniature blocks by following the step-by-step instructions as for the larger block.

3. When all the blocks are complete follow the quilt assembly instructions omitting the border strips.

4. For smaller quilts and miniatures, be sure to use low-loft wadding to give a softer drape. Binding strips are also cut narrower, to suit the smaller scale of this project.

STRAIGHT SET BEAR'S PAW

In this variation, effective use is made of plaids and stripes.
A sense of movement in the square-set blocks is achieved by varying
the direction of the fabrics. The sawtooth border with flashes of
yellow adds lightness and sparkle.

Skill level: Intermediate
Finished block: 8¾ x 8¾ in / 22.2 x 22.2 cm
Finished quilt: 36 x 36 in / 91.4 x 91.4 cm
Number of pieced blocks: 9

MATERIALS

Blue floral 1/4 yard / metre
Blue striped shirting 3/4 yard / metre
Light background 1 yard / metre
Plaid 1/3 yard / metre
Indigo print for sashing/inner border/binding
3/4 yard / metre
Backing 1/4 yard / metre
Wadding one piece 40 x 40 in / 101 x 101 cm

CUTTING INSTRUCTIONS

Indigo print

1. Cut 12 sashing strips, 2½ x 9¼ in / 6.4 x 23.5 cm.
2. Cut two strips, 2¼ x 33¾ in / 5.7 x 85.7 cm and two strips 2¼ x 37¼ in / 5.7 x 94.6 cm for the inner borders.
3. Cut four strips, 2½ in / 6.4 cm wide across the full width of the fabric for the binding.

Blue striped shirting

1. Cut nine rectangles, 6 x 10 in / 15.2 x 25.4 cm for quick-piecing the half-square A units.
2. Cut four rectangles, 6 x 12 in / 15.2 x 30.5 cm for quick-piecing the half-square units for the sawtooth border.
3. Cut 36 C squares, 1 3/4 x 1 3/4 in / 4.4 x 4.4 cm.

Plaid fabric

1. Cut 36 B squares, 3 x 3 in / 7.6 x 7.6 cm.

Light background fabric

1. Cut nine rectangles, 6 x 10 in / 15.2 x 25.4 cm for quick- piecing the half-square A units.
2. Cut five rectangles, 6 x 12 in / 15.2 x 30.5 cm for quick-piecing the half-square units for the sawtooth border.

3. Cut 36 C squares, 1¾ x 1¾ in / 4.4 x 4.4 cm.
4. Cut 36 D rectangles, 1¾ x 4¼ in / 4.4 x 10.9 cm.

Blue floral fabric

1. Cut one rectangle, 6 x 12 in / 15.2 x 30 cm for quick-piecing the half-square units for the sawtooth border.
2. Cut four squares, 2½ x 2½ in / 6.4 x 6.4 cm for the corner posts which separate the sashing strips.

PUTTING THE QUILT TOGETHER

1. Piece the nine Bear's Paw blocks according to the instructions for the large quilt set on point.
2. Sew the blocks together in three horizontal rows using sashing strips to separate the blocks.
3. Piece the remaining sashing strips into two lengths, alternating sashing strips with blue floral corner posts.
4. Sew the pieced sashing strips to the rows of blocks to make up the central section of the quilt top.
5. Sew the inner border strips to the quilt top. Press.
6. For the sawtooth border, assemble the 6 x 12 in / 15.2 x 30.5 cm rectangles into five pairs, one light and one contrast, with right sides facing. Mark a grid of 2⅛ in / 5.4 cm squares as previously described, with an extra row in order to give 20 pieced squares from each pair of rectangles.
7. Join the squares into four strips. Use the floral squares for contrast at each end and in the middle, making sure to pivot the square to follow the design.
8. Sew the sawtooth border to the quilt top.
9. Assemble the quilt layers, baste together, outline quilt and bind using the self-binding method as described in the Techniques section.

OPTICAL BEAR'S PAW

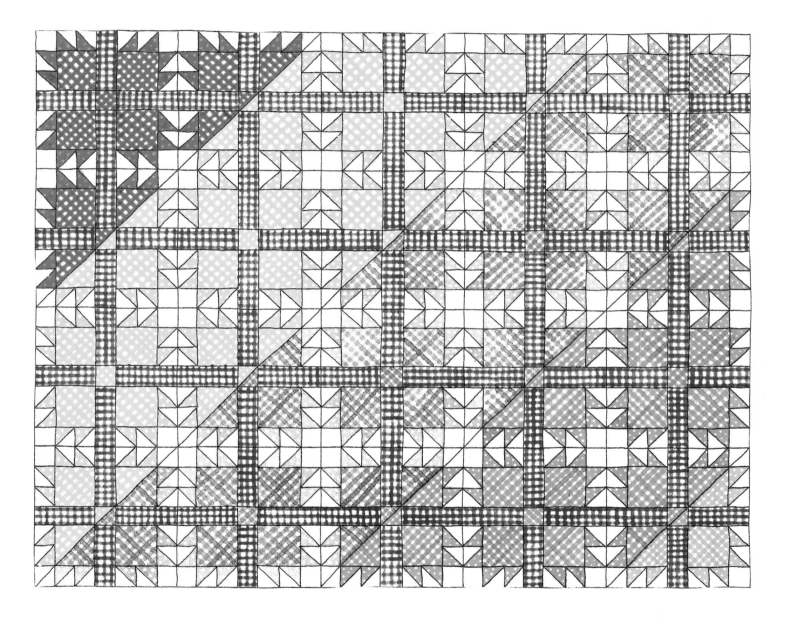

The diagonal shift of this unusual Bear's Paw variation is achieved by
careful colour placement. Each new colour strip is introduced by dividing the
block into two colour halves. By using a light contrast colour for the
small trianglular-shaped 'claws', a secondary pattern of
intersecting 'flying geese' emerges.

Mennonite Baskets

BASKETS

The basket is an enduringly popular design and has withstood
the vagaries of changing quilt fashion. In the mid-nineteenth century
the basket was an ornate, flower-filled appliqué motif - standard on
all album quilts. It was successfully adapted when the demand for
appliqué quilts diminished and was replaced by pieced geometric
designs. This lively Mennonite quilt has been simply pieced from
triangles and diamonds in turkey red and chrome yellow,
a favourite palette of mid-nineteenth century quilters.

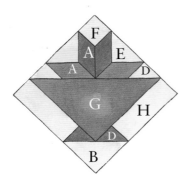

Skill level: Intermediate
Finished quilt: 73 x 80 in / 185.4 x 203.2 cm
Finished block: 10 x 10 in / 25.4 x 25.4 cm
Number of blocks: 20

MATERIALS

Cream 3 yards / metres
Red 2¹/₂ yards / metres
Orange 1¹/₂ yards / metres
Wadding 77 x 84 in / 195.6 x 213.4 cm
Backing 4¹/₄ yards / metres

CUTTING INSTRUCTIONS

Note: Prepare Template A, provided with variations 1 and 2. Use the measurements to cut pieces B, D, E, F, G, and H.

Red fabric
1. Cut two strips, 5 x 83 in / 12.7 x 210.8 cm and one strip 5 x 75 in / 12.7 x 190.5 cm for the borders.
2. Cut two binding strips, 2¹/₂ x 83 in / 6.4 x 210.8 cm, and two strips, 2¹/₂ x 76 in / 6.4 x 193 cm.
3. Cut 10 squares, 8⁷/₈ x 8⁷/₈ in / 22.5 x 22.5 cm. Cut diagonally in half to make 20 G triangles.
4. Cut 20 squares, 2⁷/₈ x 2⁷/₈ in / 7.3 x 7.3 cm. Cut diagonally in half to make make 40 D triangles.
5. Using Template A, cut 20 pieces. Reverse the template and cut 20 more.

Orange fabric
1. Cut two border strips, 6 x 83 in / 15.2 x 210.8 cm, and one strip 6 x 75 in / 15.2 x 190.5 cm, joining as necessary.
2. Using Template A, cut 20 pieces. Reverse the template and cut 20 more.

Cream fabric
1. Cut two border strips, 3 x 83 in / 7.6 x 210.8 cm and one strip, 3 x 76 in / 7.6 x 193 cm.
2. Cut 12 setting squares, 10¹/₂ x 10¹/₂ in / 26.7 x 26.7 cm.
3. Cut three squares, 15¹/₂ x 15¹/₂ in / 39.4 x 39.4 cm. Cut across both diagonals to make 12 side triangles. Use one of these triangles as a template and cut two more, making sure that the straight grain runs parallel with the longest side.
4. Cut two squares, 8 x 8 in / 20.3 x 20.3 cm. Cut diagonally in half to make 4 corner triangles.
5. Cut ten squares, 4⁷/₈ x 4⁷/₈ in / 12.4 x 12.4 cm diagonally in half to make 20 B triangles.
6. Cut 20 squares, 2⁷/₈ x 2⁷/₈ in / 7.3 x 7.3 cm. Cut diagonally in half to make 40 D triangles.
7. Cut 10 squares, 5¹/₄ x 5¹/₄ in / 13.3 x 13.3 cm. Cut across both diagonals to make 40 E triangles.
8. Cut 20 F squares, 2¹/₂ x 2¹/₂ in / 6.4 x 6.4 cm.
9. Cut seven strips, 2¹/₂ in / 6.4 cm wide across the full width of the fabric. Cut into 40 H rectangles, 2¹/₂ x 6¹/₂ in / 6.4 x 16.5 cm.

PIECING THE BLOCKS

1. Stitch a red A to an orange A. Repeat to make two pairs.

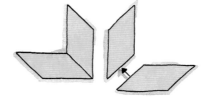

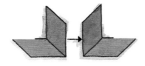

2. Join the pairs together along the red edges. Press.

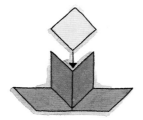
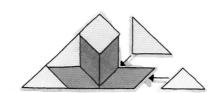

3. Inset an F square, and two E triangles. Add two cream D triangles to complete the top half of the block.

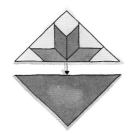

4. Stitch a G triangle to the base of the pieced unit.

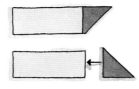

5. Sew a red D triangle to an H rectangle. Make another D/H unit, but reverse the D triangle. Press.

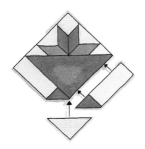

6. Sew a D/H piece to each side of the G triangle. Press, then sew a cream B triangle to complete the block.

7. Make another 19 blocks following the same instructions.

PUTTING THE BLOCKS TOGETHER

1. Arrange the basket blocks alternately with the cream squares. Place side and corner triangles at each end of the diagonal rows in the correct positions.

2. Stitch the blocks together in diagonal rows, pressing seams towards the pieced blocks.

3. Stitch the rows of blocks together matching points between blocks.

ADDING THE BORDERS

1. Mark the cutting line along the length of the red border strips using the wavy line template, and cut the edge of the red borders to shape.

2. Turn a narrow hem on the shaped edges and blind hem the red border onto the orange border strip, overlapping by 3 in / 7.6 cm. The double border should measure 8¼ in / 21 cm wide.

3. Refer to the main illustration and stitch the appliqué borders to the two long sides of the centre panel, trimming to fit. Then, stitch the shorter piece along the bottom edge, once again trimming to fit. Press seams towards the borders.

4. Repeat with the 3 in / 7.6 cm cream border strips.

QUILTING AND FINISHING

1. Give the quilt top a final press on the back and front. Trim away any loose threads which may show through to the front.

2. From the quilting patterns supplied, mark a design to the plain setting squares using your preferred method. Straight line quilting such as grid or contour quilting can be marked with ¼ in / 6 mm masking tape, or worked by eye as you quilt.

3. Assemble the quilt layers and baste in a grid.

4. Quilt, working from the centre outwards.

5. When quilting is complete, use the binding strips to finish the edges with straight binding as directed in the Techniques section.

CAKE STAND

In Cake Stand, pure solid colours are combined with black giving an 'Art Deco' look to the quilt.

Skill level: Intermediate
Finished quilt: 47 x 58 in / 119.3 x 147.3 cm
Finished block: 8 x 8 in / 20.3 x 20.3 cm
Number of blocks: 12

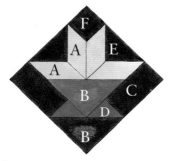

MATERIALS

Dark blue 1³/4 yards / metres
Black ³/4 yard / metre
Cream ³/4 yard / metre
Orange, green, red, pink and bright blue 1/4 yard / metre each
Wadding 49 x 61 in / 124.6 x 154.9 cm
Backing / binding 2³/4 yards / metres

CUTTING INSTRUCTIONS

Trace and prepare templates according to the instructions in the Techniques section.

Dark blue fabric

1. Cut two strips, 4 x 45 in / 10.2 x 114.3 cm and two strips 4 x 63 in / 10.2 x 160 cm for borders.
2. Cut six setting squares, 8¹/2 x 8¹/2 in / 21.6 x 21.6 cm.
3. Cut three squares, 12⁵/8 x 12⁵/8 in / 32 x 32 cm. Cut across both diagonals to make 12 side triangles.
4. Cut two squares, 6⁵/8 x 6⁵/8 in / 16.8 x 16.8 cm. Cut diagonally in half to make 4 corner triangles.

Black fabric

1. Using the relevant templates, cut 12 B and 24 E triangles, 24 C rectangles, and 12 F squares.

Pink fabric

1. Using template A, cut eight pieces. Reverse the template and cut eight more to get a mirror image.

Cream fabric

1. Using template A, cut 16 pieces. Reverse the template and cut 16 more.
2. Cut two strips, 2 x 40 in / 5.1 x 101.6 cm and two strips, 2 x 54 in / 5.1 x 137.1 cm for borders. Join if necessary to make up the lengths. Borders are generous to allow for trimming to fit.

Orange fabric

1. Using the relevant templates, cut eight B and 16 D triangles.

Bright blue fabric

1. Using the templates, cut four B and eight D triangles.

Green fabric

1. Cut two border strips, 2 x 36 in / 5.1 x 91.4 cm.

Red fabric

1. Cut two border strips, 2 x 52 in / 5.1 x 132 cm. Join if necessary to make up the lengths.

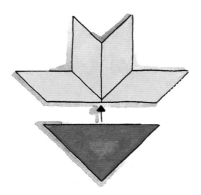

PIECING THE BLOCKS

1. Following the piecing diagram, sew four A pieces together. Press, then add on a blue or orange B triangle. Press.

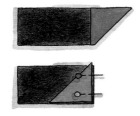

2. Sew a blue or orange D triangle to a C rectangle. Repeat, changing the orientation of the D triangle. Press.

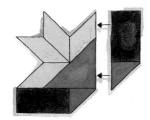

3. Sew the C/D pieces to two sides of the basket.

4. Sew on a black B triangle to form the base of the basket.

5. Inset one F square and two E triangles to complete the block.

6. Make 11 more blocks referring to the main illustration for colour placement.

PUTTING THE BLOCKS TOGETHER

1. Arrange the pieced blocks alternately with the plain blue squares, placing side and corner triangles at each end of the diagonal rows in the correct positions.

2. Stitch the blocks together in diagonal rows, pressing seams towards the plain blocks.

3. Stitch the rows of blocks together matching points between blocks.

ADDING THE BORDERS

1. Add the borders in sequence, trimming the lengths to fit as you work. Press seams towards the borders.

QUILTING AND FINISHING

1. Give the quilt top a final press and trim away any loose ends.

2. Mark the quilting pattern on the border using your preferred method. The grid pattern in the centre panel can be marked as you work with 1/4 in / 6 mm masking tape.

3. Assemble the quilt layers and baste in a grid.

4. Quilt working from the centre outwards.

5. Use the self-binding method to finish the raw edges of the quilt by bringing the backing over and slipstitching to the front.

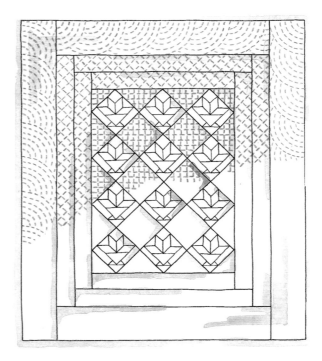

AUTUMN BASKETS

In this variation, the same block makes a radically different quilt when the colour scheme is changed, prints are used and the blocks are turned and set together in a different way.

Skill level: Intermediate
Quilt size: 55 x 77 in / 139.7 x 195.6 cm
Finished block: 8 x 8 in / 20.3 x 20.3 cm
Number of blocks: 24

MATERIALS

Indigo print 2¼ yards / metres
White 2 yards / metres
Acid green ½ yard / metre
Pale brown print ½ yard / metre
Dark brown print ½ yard / metre
Wadding 59 x 81 in / 149.9 x 205.7 cm
Backing 3½ yards / metres

CUTTING INSTRUCTIONS

Trace and prepare the same templates as for 'Cake Stand'.

Indigo print
1. Cut two strips, 2½ x 77 in / 6.4 x 195.6 cm, and two strips 2½ x 59 in / 6.4 x 149.9 cm, for the borders. Excess length has been allowed for trimming to fit.
2. Cut 15 setting squares, 8½ x 8½ in / 21.6 x 21.6 cm.
3. Cut four squares, 15½ x 15½ in / 39.3 x 39.3 cm. Cut across both diagonals to make 16 side triangles.
4. Cut two squares, 8 x 8 in / 20.3 x 20.3 cm. Cut diagonally in half to make four corner triangles.

White fabric
1. Cut two strips, 3 x 71 in / 7.6 x 180.3 cm, and two strips, 3 x 49 in / 7.6 x 124.4 cm for the borders.
2. Using the relevant templates, cut 48 C rectangles, 24 B and 48 E triangles and 24 F squares.

Acid green fabric
1. Using template A, cut 24 pieces. Reverse the template, and cut 24 more A pieces.

Pale brown print fabric
1. Using template A, cut 24 pieces. Reverse the template, and cut 24 more A pieces.

Dark brown print fabric
1. Using the relevant templates, cut 24 B and 48 D triangles.

PIECING THE BLOCKS

1. Follow the same piecing directions as for 'Cake Stand'.
2. Make a total of 24 blocks.

PUTTING THE BLOCKS TOGETHER

1. Arrange the pieced blocks alternately with the plain blocks, placing side and corner triangles at each end of the diagonal rows in the correct positions.
2. Stitch the blocks together in diagonal rows, pressing seams towards the plain blocks.
3. Stitch the rows of blocks together, matching points between blocks.

ADDING THE BORDERS

1. Sew the two shorter white border strips to the top and bottom of the quilt. Press, then add the two side border strips.
2. Add the indigo print borders following the same sequence.

QUILTING AND FINISHING

1. Follow the same procedure for marking, assembling the quilt layers, basting, quilting and binding as instructed for 'Cake Stand'.

CROSS AND CROWN

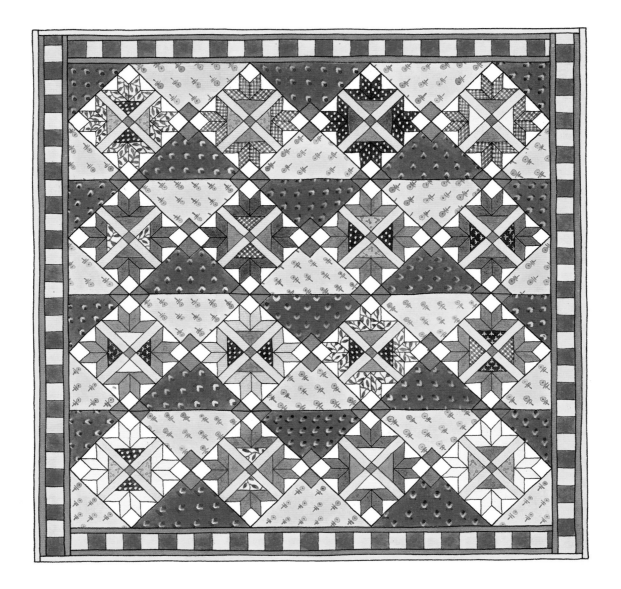

A riot of primary colours is used in the final variation. The basket blocks, set on point in sets of four are separated by narrow yellow sashing with a small square in the centre. With alternating blocks made of two large triangles, the baskets are ingeniously linked by a small four-patch with a square at the corner of each connecting block. The red, blue and yellow border emphasizes this high-spirited composition.

Amish Diamond in a Square

DIAMOND IN A SQUARE

The Diamond in a Square is one of the most popular of Amish designs. The large shapes which make up the quilt top and the simple piecing arrangement provide an ideal vehicle for displaying elaborate quilting patterns. Although religious codes in many Amish communities restricted needlework choices to simple, non-representational designs in plain coloured fabric, Amish women decorated their quilts with a panoply of ornate and sensuous designs.

The main quilt in this set displays a central quilting motif consisting of a radiating eight-pointed star surrounded by a feather wreath and backed with a cross-hatched grid. This is complemented by pumpkin seed and looped, running feather border designs. Close quilting creates the richly textured pattern on the surface so prized by quilt devotees.

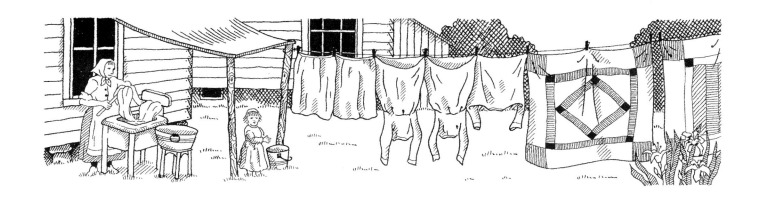

Skill level: Intermediate
Finished quilt: 78 x 78 in / 198.1 x 198.1 cm

MATERIALS

Red ³/4 yard / metre
Pink 1³/8 yards / metres
Green 1¹/2 yards /metres
Purple 2³/4 yards / metres
Wadding 80 x 80 in / 203.2 x 203.2 cm
Backing 4¹/2 yards / metres
Binding ³/4 yard / metre

CUTTING INSTRUCTIONS

It is not necessary to make templates for this project. It can be easily and quickly cut with a rotary cutter and quilter's ruler. All measurements include the necessary ¹/4 in / 6 mm seam allowances.

Red fabric
1. Cut one central square, 25¹/4 x 25¹/4 in / 64.1 x 64.1 cm.
2. Cut four squares, 4¹/2 x 4¹/2 in / 11.4 x 11.4 cm for the inner corner posts.

Pink fabric
1. Cut four strips, 4¹/2 x 46¹/2 in / 11.4 x 118.1 cm, and four strips, 4¹/2 x 25¹/4 in / 11.4 x 64.1 cm for the inner borders.

Green fabric
1. Cut two squares, 23⁷/8 x 23⁷/8 in / 60.6 x 60.6 cm. Cut in half across the diagonal to make four corner triangles.
2. Cut four corner posts, 12¹/2 x 12¹/2 in / 31.8 x 31.8 cm.

Purple fabric
1. Cut four strips, 12¹/2 x 46¹/2 in / 31.8 x 118.1 cm for the outer border.

Binding
1. Cut eight strips, 2¹/2 in / 6.4 cm wide across the full width of the fabric.

PIECING THE QUILT TOP

1. Stitch two short pink border strips to either side of the central red square. Press seam allowances towards the red.

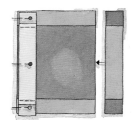

2. Stitch a red corner post to each end of the remaining two short pink inner border strips. Press towards the red posts, then sew on to the central red square, taking care to match points.

3. Pin, then sew the long side of two green triangles to opposite sides of the centre unit, matching the ¹/4 in / 6 mm seam allowances at the ends and taking great care not to stretch the edges of the triangles. Ease them onto the straight pink / red strips. Press without stretching.

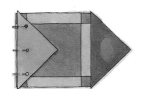

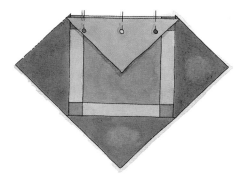

4. Similarly, attach the remaining two triangles to the other two sides of the centre.

5. Join two longer pink border strips to opposite sides of the centre unit and press towards the green.

6. Stitch a small green corner post to opposite ends of the remaining two pink border strips and press towards the green. Attach to the top and bottom of the centre panel.

7. Attach two purple strips to the sides of the centre panel and press towards the purple.

8. Stitch a large green corner post to both ends of the remaining two purple strips and press towards the purple.

9. Attach these strips to the top and bottom of the centre panel and press towards the purple.

QUILTING AND FINISHING

1. Press the quilt carefully. Trim away any loose threads which may show through to the front.

2. From the quilting patterns supplied, mark a pumpkin seed pattern in the pink borders, eight-pointed stars in the small corner posts, feathers in the purple borders and U-shaped feather wreaths in the large corner posts. The diamond grid in the green triangles can be marked as you work with 1/4 in / 6 mm masking tape.

3. Divide the backing fabric in half. Place right sides together with selvedges matching and stitch, parallel to one edge taking a 1/2 in / 1.3 cm seam. Trim away the selvedge and press.

4. Assemble the quilt layers and baste in a grid.

5. Quilt, working from the centre outwards.

6. Trim the edges of the quilt to prepare for binding.

7. Join the binding strips as necessary, then apply a straight binding as directed in the Techniques section.

SPOOLS

Although a large quilt, this project is simple to piece using
a quick-triangle method for the centre blocks and a traditional
template-free approach called 'Hit and Miss' for the borders.

Skill level: Easy
Finished quilt: 96 x 96 in / 243.8 x 243.8 cm
Finished centre block: 12 x 12 in / 30.5 x 30.5 cm

MATERIALS

Dark forest green 1/2 yard / metre
Dusty pink a fat quarter (a piece 18 x 22 in / 45.7 x 55.9 cm)
Slate green a fat quarter
Assorted solid fabrics to total 7 yards / metres
Wadding 98 x 98 in / 249 x 249 cm
Backing 81/4 yards / metres

CUTTING INSTRUCTIONS

1. The measurements of this quilt mean that the backing fabric must be cut into three equal lengths. These are seamed parallel to the selvedges with a 1/2 in / 1.3 cm seam allowance. Trim away the selvedges and press, then cut a square, 99 x 99 in / 251.5 x 251.5 cm for the backing, centred over the seams. If this is done first the remaining fabric can be incorporated into the amount required for the border piecing. The excess is approximately equivalent to 27 in x 23/4 yards / 68.6 cm x 2.75 metres.

2. For cutting the border 'bricks', see Adding the Borders section.

PIECING THE BLOCKS FOR THE CENTRE MEDALLION

1. On the wrong side of the dusty pink fabric, mark a square, 131/4 x 131/4 in / 33.7 x 33.7 cm and one diagonal line. Place right sides together with the dark forest green fabric and cut out leaving a 2 in / 5.1 cm border all around the square.

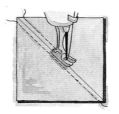

2. Machine-stitch 1/4 in / 6 mm on both sides of the diagonal line. Press, then cut out the square and cut along the diagonal pencil line. Open to create two pieced squares and press the seams towards the darker fabric.

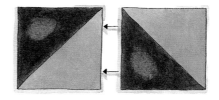

3. Place these two squares right sides together once again, having the pink triangle on one side facing the dark green triangle on the other. Mark the 'missing' diagonal then stitch on both sides of this line as before. Press, then cut apart as before to obtain two identical squares of pieced quarter triangles.

4. Repeat the whole operation, substituting the slate green for the pink fabric.

5. Arrange the four blocks in a pinwheel and stitch them together in pairs. Press, then join the pairs to form the centre medallion.

ADDING THE BORDERS

1. The framing strips of this quilt are worked using a method called 'Hit and Miss'. All the patches in the strip are the same width but they vary in length and form no particular pattern. Sometimes they appear like bricks, other times they may be squares or even narrower than the width of the finished strip. Do not worry about where the joins will come on neighbouring rows. Sometimes they coincide, but more often they 'miss', hence the name.

2. Make up sets of strips as listed below and use the lettered piecing plan for the sewing order:

Set B: two strips, 6¹/₂ x 24¹/₂ in / 16.5 x 62.2 cm
Set C: two strips, 6¹/₂ x 36¹/₂ in / 16.5 x 92.7 cm
Set D: two strips, 6¹/₂ x 36¹/₂ in / 16.5 x 92.7 cm
Set E: two strips, 6¹/₂ x 48¹/₂ in / 16.5 x 123.2 cm
Set F: two strips, 8 ¹/₂ x 48¹/₂ in / 21.6 x 123.2 cm
Set G: four strips, 6¹/₂ x 64¹/₂ in / 16.5 x 163.8 cm
Set H: four strips, 8¹/₂ x 72¹/₂ in / 21.6 x 184.1 cm
Set J: two strips, 12¹/₂ x 96¹/₂ in / 31.7 x 245.1 cm

3. Attach these strips in alphabetical order.

QUILTING AND FINISHING

1. Press the quilt top from the front and back. Trim away any loose threads which may show through.
2. From the quilting patterns provided select one or more that complement your colour arrangement. Combine designs to create an overall pattern.
3. Layer the backing, wadding and quilt top and baste in a grid.
4. Quilt, working from the centre outwards.
5. When quilting is complete, finish the edges with a self-binding by folding the backing fabric over to the front of the quilt and hemming, as directed in the Techniques section.

CRISS-CROSS DIAMONDS

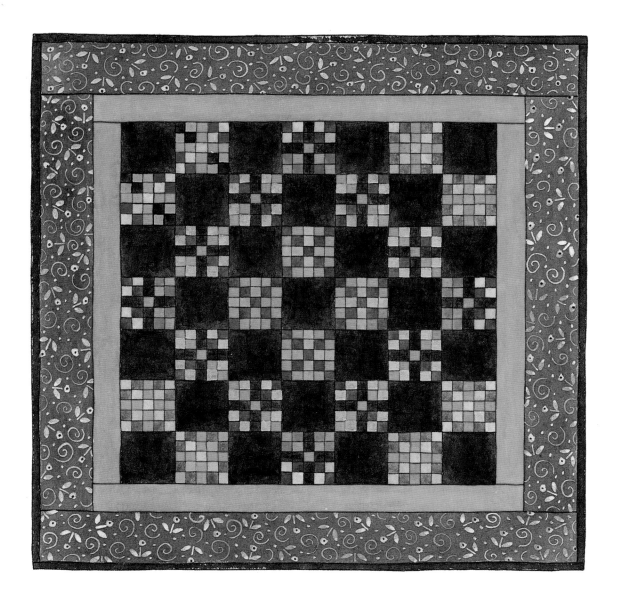

By careful placement of blocks, the red centres of the
nine-patch blocks create a diamond outline.

Skill level: Intermediate
Finished quilt: 100 x 100 in / 254 x 254 cm
Finished block: 10 x 10 in / 25.4 x 25.4 cm
Number of blocks: 24

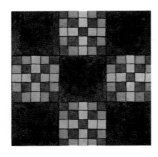

MATERIALS

Black 2³/8 yards / metres
Scarlet red 2¹/4 yards / metres
Purple ¹/2 yard / metre
Purple print for outer border 2³/4 yards / metres
Pale blue ¹/2 yard / metre
Beige ³/8 yard / metre
Bright blue ¹/8 yard / metre
Brown ¹/4 yard / metre
Lilac ¹/8 yard / metre
Wadding 104 x 104 in / 264.2 x 264.2 cm
Backing 8³/4 yards / metres

CUTTING INSTRUCTIONS

Black fabric
1. Cut 25 squares, 10¹/2 x 10¹/2 in / 26.7 x 26.7 cm.
2. Cut 48 rectangles, 2¹/2 x 4¹/2 in / 6.4 x 11.4 cm.
3. Cut eight squares, 2¹/2 x 2¹/2 in / 6.4 x 6.4 cm.
4. Cut ten binding strips, 2¹/2 in / 6.4 cm wide across the width of the fabric.

Scarlet red fabric
1. Cut two border strips, 5 x 81 in / 12.7 x 205.7 cm, and two border strips, 5 x 72¹/2 in / 12.7 x 184.1 cm. Note that these measurements are generous to allow for trimming to fit.
2. Cut 32 rectangles, 2¹/2 x 4¹/2 in / 6.4 x 11.4 cm.
3. Cut 92 squares, 2¹/2 x 2¹/2 in / 6.4 x 6.4 cm.

Purple fabric
1. Cut 92 squares, 2¹/2 x 2¹/2 in / 6.4 x 6.4 cm.

Purple print fabric
1. Cut nine strips, 10¹/2 in / 26.7 cm wide across the full width of the fabric. Join to make two strips, 81 in / 205.7 cm long, and two strips, 102 in / 259 cm for outer borders.

Pale blue fabric
1. Cut 16 rectangles, 2¹/2 x 4¹/2 in / 6.4 x 11.4 cm.
2. Cut 56 squares, 2¹/2 x 2¹/2 in / 6.4 x 6.4 cm.

Beige fabric
1. Cut 84 squares, 2¹/2 x 2¹/2 in / 6.4 x 6.4 cm.

Bright blue fabric
1. Cut 16 squares, 2¹/2 x 2¹/2 in / 6.4 x 6.4 cm.

Brown fabric
1. Cut 48 squares, 2¹/2 x 2¹/2 in / 6.4 x 6.4 cm.

Lilac fabric
1. Cut 12 squares, 2¹/2 x 2¹/2 in / 6.4 x 6.4 cm.

PIECING THE BLOCKS

All the pieced blocks in this quilt are the same construction but they are coloured differently. Follow the instructions for piecing Block A, then work the remaining blocks making the appropriate colour substitutions.

Block A   Block B

   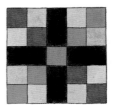

Block C   Block D

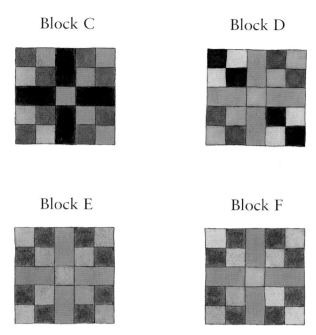

Block E   Block F

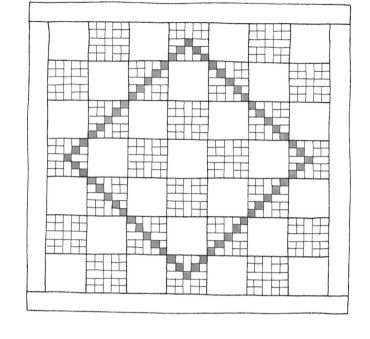

1. Stitch eight scarlet and eight purple squares together in pairs. Press seams to one side then stitch two pairs together in a chequerboard arrangement to make four, four-patch units.

2. Stitch a four-patch unit to opposite sides of a pale blue rectangle for the top half of the block. Repeat for the bottom half of the block.

3. Stitch a pale blue rectangle to opposite sides of a central purple square. Press all seams, then stitch all three assembled strips together to complete the block. Work a total of four A blocks.

4. In the same manner make eight Block B, four Block C, two Block D, three Block E, and three Block F.

PUTTING THE BLOCKS TOGETHER

1. On a flat surface, arrange the blocks alternating black setting squares with pieced blocks. Special attention must be paid to the direction of the strongly coloured diagonal rows of squares in each block for the pattern to appear correctly.

2. Stitch the blocks together in rows, pressing the seams in opposite directions on alternate rows, then join the rows together to complete the centre panel.

ADDING THE BORDERS

1. Add a shorter red border strip to opposite sides of the quilt. Press.

2. Stitch the remaining longer strips to the top and bottom of the quilt.

3. Repeat the sequence with the purple print borders.

QUILTING AND FINISHING

1. Press the quilt top carefully from the front and back.

2. Mark the top with a quilting design of your choice. A single large motif will work well in the plain black setting blocks and a pumpkin seed motif worked in each little square will emphasize the diagonal movement of the piecing. Use a slightly larger pumpkin seed design in the border to frame the centre.

3. Divide the backing fabric in thirds. With right sides together and selvedges matching, stitch the panels together along the selvedges taking

$1/2$ in / 1.3 cm seam allowance. Trim away the selvedges and press.

4. Layer the backing, wadding and quilt top together and baste in a grid.

5. Work the quilting design from the centre outwards.

6. When quilting is complete, join the binding strips as necessary to make the required lengths and finish the edges with a folded straight binding as directed in the Techniques section.

PYRAMIDS

A successful formula for making effective scrap quilts is to manipulate
the tonal values of the fabrics by separating and ordering the light and dark
fabrics. The last quilt in this set employs this device with great success.
Radiating bands of triangles in a multitude of light and dark fabrics
shift and combine to form large and small diamonds.

Mennonite Straight Furrows

LOG CABIN

The strength of the Log Cabin design is its versatility. So many different patterns can be made by arranging the blocks in different combinations. A single block is quite straightforward - strips of fabric rotate around a centre square with the tonal values split diagonally into dark and light. Traditionally, log cabin blocks are stitched to a foundation of calico plain cotton. This stabilises the block and conceals the seams on the back. Many log cabin quilts have no extra filling layer, as the foundation itself provides enough insulation between the top pieced layer and the backing. The first quilt in this set is called Straight Furrows for the blocks have been arranged to create a pattern of straight diagonal lines.

Skill level: Easy
Finished quilt: 70 x 70 in / 177.8 x 177.8 cm
Finished block: 7¼ x 7¼ in / 18.4 x 18.4 cm
Number of blocks: 64

MATERIALS

Plain calico for foundation fabric 5 yards / metres
Pale blue ¼ yard / metre
Brown 3 yards / metres
Cream 3 yards / metres
Wadding (optional) 72 x 72 in / 182.9 x 182.9 cm
Backing fabric 4½ yards / metres

CUTTING INSTRUCTIONS

Brown fabric
1. Cut two strips, 2½ x 62 in / 6.4 x 157.5 cm for side borders.
2. Cut four strips, 2½ x 74 in / 6.4 x 188 cm for top and bottom borders.
3. Cut four strips, 2½ x 73 in / 6.4 x 185.4 cm for binding.
4. Cut 1 in / 2.5 cm strips from the remaining fabric for the block strips, cutting from the remaining length left from the borders, then across the width from selvedge to selvedge.

Cream fabric
1. Cut four strips, 2½ x 62 in / 6.4 x 157.4 cm for side borders.
2. Cut two strips, 2½ x 74 in / 6.4 x 188 cm for top and bottom borders.
3. Cut 1 in / 2.5 cm strips from the remaining fabric for the block strips, cutting across the width from selvedge to selvedge.

Pale blue fabric
1. Cut 64 squares 1¾ x 1¾ in / 4.4 x 4.4 cm for the centres of the blocks.

Foundation fabric
1. Cut two strips, 6½ x 62 in / 16.5 x 157.5 cm for the side border backing.
2. Cut two strips 6½ x 74 in / 16.5 x 188 cm, for the top and bottom border backing. Extra length is included to allow for trimming to fit.
3. Cut 68 squares, 8½ x 8½ in / 21.6 x 21.6 cm for backing the blocks.

Sample block
1. You will need one square of foundation fabric, one pale blue square and a total length of 1 x 54 in / 2.5 x 137.2 cm brown and 1 x 48 in / 2.5 x 121.9 cm cream fabric for the strips.

PIECING THE BLOCKS

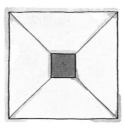

1. Prepare the foundation squares by marking two diagonal lines from corner to corner. Then, position the blue square right side up in the centre, lining up the corners with the marked line.

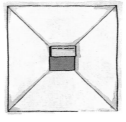

2. Take a strip of the cream fabric and cut a length to fit one side of the square. Place this right side down along one

side of the centre square, pin and stitch through all three layers - strip, centre and foundation fabric - with a ¼ in / 6 mm seam allowance.

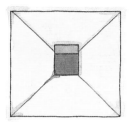

3. Flip the strip over to reveal the right side of the fabric and press flat against the foundation.

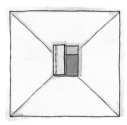

4. Cut another length from the cream fabric to fit along the next side of the centre and the short edge of the first strip. Place this second strip right side down and stitch through all three layers as before.

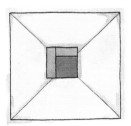

5. Flip the strip over as before to lie flat against the foundation, revealing the right side of the fabric and press.

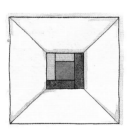

6. Add strips of the brown fabric to the third and fourth sides of the centre square in the same way, placing right side down and stitching, then flipping over and pressing flat against the foundation.

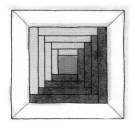

7. Continue to add strips of cream and brown keeping the light/dark sequence correct and increasing the

length of each strip to fit. Be careful not to change direction as you work. To avoid confusion you can draw a small arrow on the foundation square for reference.

8. When six rounds of strips have been stitched down, trim away the excess foundation fabric even with the outer edges of the final round. The block should measure 7¾ in / 19.7 cm square, including the ¼ in / 6 mm seam allowance for joining the blocks together.

9. Baste the outer edge of the pieced block to the foundation within the seam allowance.

10. Make 63 more blocks following the same sequence.

PUTTING THE BLOCKS TOGETHER

1. Refer to the main illustration and arrange the blocks to form the 'Straight Furrow' design. Stitch the blocks together through both layers. Sew first into sets of two, then four, eight, 16 and finally four sets of 16 into the 64 blocks which make up the centre panel, easing to fit where necessary.
2. Press the seams open as you work so that the double thickness of the pieced top and the foundation becomes as flat as possible.

ADDING THE BORDERS

1. For the side borders, stitch two shorter cream strips to either side of the shorter brown strips. Press.
2. Take the two shorter calico strips and attach these to the wrong side of the side borders by steam pressing the fabrics together then pinning or basting the two layers.

3. Treat these two layers of fabric as one and stitch the side borders to the opposite sides of the centre panel. Trim the length of the borders even with the edges and press.

4. Make up the top and bottom borders by sewing the brown strips to either side of the cream strips. Back these pieced borders with calico as for the side borders. Sew these to the top and bottom of the quilt; trim even with the sides and press.

QUILTING AND FINISHING

1. Press the quilt carefully and trim away any loose threads which may show through to the front.

2. Transfer the double cable quilting pattern to the borders using your preferred method. Straight line quilting follows the log cabin strips. This can be marked as you work after layering or done by eye.

3. Assemble the quilt layers and baste in a grid.

4. Quilt from the centre outwards finishing with the border cables.

5. When quilting is complete, finish the raw edges of the quilt with the prepared binding strips, as directed in the Techniques section.

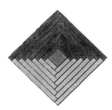

COURTHOUSE STEPS

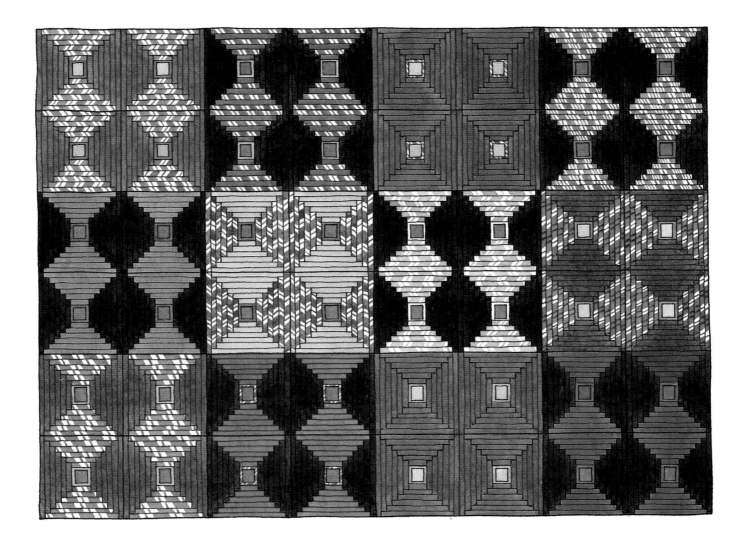

In the Courthouse Steps variation of the Log Cabin design, contrasting strips are set opposite each other rather than in spiral formation. In this bold version an original touch is added by framing the block centres with a contrasting fabric before the strips are added.

Skill level: Easy
Finished quilt: 72 x 96 in / 182.8 x 243.8 cm
Finished block: 12 x 12 in / 30.5 x 30.5 cm
Number of blocks: 48

MATERIALS

The first figures refer to a set of four blocks, those in brackets refer to the total 48 blocks:

Assorted scraps for centre squares 5 x 5 in / 12.7 x 12.7 cm (¼ yard / metre)

Contrasting strip for centre square frame 1 x 48 in / 2.5 x 122 cm (½ yard / metre)

Dark fabric ½ yard / metre (6 yards / metres)

Light fabric ½ yard / metre (6 yards / metres)

Plain calico for foundation fabric (optional) 6¼ yards / metres

Wadding (optional) 76 x 100 in / 193 x 254 cm

Backing / binding 5½ yards / metres

CUTTING INSTRUCTIONS

Although log cabin quilts were traditionally pieced onto a foundation, the larger block size used here can be pieced without a foundation.

1. If you are using the foundation method, cut 48 squares, 14 x 14 in / 35.6 x 35.6 cm from the foundation fabric.

2. For each set of four blocks, cut four centre squares, 2½ x 2½ in / 6.4 x 6.4 cm; cut 48 for the entire quilt.

3. For each set of four blocks, cut eight centre frame strips, 1 x 2½ in / 2.5 x 6.4 cm and eight strips 1 x 3½ in / 2.5 x 8.9 cm. You will need 96 strips of each length for the entire quilt.

4. For each set of four blocks, cut an assortment of strips from light and dark fabrics, 1½ in / 3.2 cm wide. The correct length for each strip can be cut to fit as you work.

PIECING THE BLOCKS

1. If you are using foundation squares, prepare them by marking two diagonal line in the same way as for the 'Straight Furrow' quilt.

2. Add the frame strips to the centre square. Then, build up the log cabin with the contrasting fabric strips opposite each other, starting with the dark fabric.

3. If you are using a foundation, use the same method as directed for the 'Straight Furrow' design, placing strips right side down, stitching and flipping over to reveal the right side of the fabric then pressing flat against the foundation fabric.

4. If you are not using foundation fabric, then place fabric right sides together and stitch, using a standard ¼ in / 6 mm seam allowance. Press seams away from the centre.

5. When the block has six rounds of strips in addition to the centre frame, trim the foundation fabric (if used) and baste the layers together. The block should measure 12½ in / 31.8 cm square including the seam allowance for joining the blocks.

PUTTING THE BLOCKS TOGETHER

1. Using the illustration as a guide, arrange and sew blocks together in sets of four. Then, stitch three rows of four blocks each. Finally stitch the rows together.

QUILTING AND FINISHING

1. Press the quilt top well on the back and front, trimming away any loose threads.

2. If you wish to use wadding, assemble the three layers together and baste in a grid.

3. If the quilt top is pieced onto a foundation, smooth onto the backing, positioning the quilt top in the centre to allow enough of the backing to project all round the outer edges to allow for self-binding.

4. Quilt in straight lines following the log cabin strips. These can be marked as you work with 1/4 in / 6 mm masking tape or measured by eye.

5. When quilting is complete, finish the raw edges with self-binding, as described in the Techniques section.

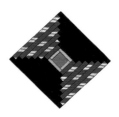

MINIATURE BARN RAISING

Barn Raising, another popular Log Cabin variation is made here as a scrap quilt
in miniature. Accuracy on a small scale is achieved by taking the foundation piecing
method a step further, and stitching from the back onto a pre-drawn miniature block
on the foundation fabric. When you choose your fabrics, make sure that you have
plenty of contrast between light and dark. For an old-fashioned look,
choose small prints, checks, pin dots, florals and geometric patterns.

Skill level: Intermediate
Finished quilt: 20 x 20 in / 50.8 x 50.8 cm
Finished block: 3 x 3 in / 7.6 x 7.6 cm
Number of blocks: 36

MATERIALS

Plain cotton or calico for foundation ¾ yard / metre
Red fabric 15 x 15 in / 38.1 x 38.1 cm
Assorted small scraps in dark and light values
each at least 2 x 3½ in / 5.1 x 8.9 cm
Backing 24 x 24 in / 61 x 61 cm
Binding ¼ yard / metre

CUTTING INSTRUCTIONS

1. From the plain calico, cut 36 squares, 4 x 4 in /
10.2 x 10.2 cm for the foundation.
2. From the red fabric, cut 36 centre squares, 1 x 1
in / 2.5 x 2.5 cm.
3. For the blocks, cut approximately 420 strips,
each 1 in / 2.5 cm wide from the assortment of
light and dark scraps.
4. From the assorted scraps, cut 36 strips, 2 x 3½
in / 5.1 x 8.9 cm for the borders and four corner
posts, 2 x 2 in / 5.1 x 5.1 cm.
5. Cut three strips, 1½ in / 3.8 cm across the full
width of the fabric for binding.

PIECING THE BLOCKS

1. First prepare the foundation. Trace the block
onto graph paper with an embroidery transfer
pencil. Keep the point sharp as you work to
produce a fine line. Follow the manufacturer's
instructions for the pencil and transfer the design
onto the foundation squares. One drawing will
produce four impressions. You can buy pre-

stamped panels from quilting suppliers, but this
means that you are restricted to the available sizes.
Drawing your own means you have the freedom to
reduce or enlarge the block and choose the number
of 'log' rounds.

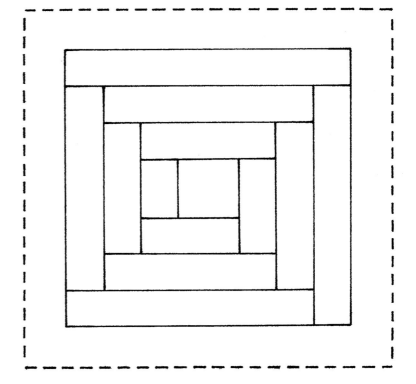

2. Place a centre red square right side up in the
centre of the foundation on the blank side (the
opposite side from which you have marked the
design.) You may have to hold the foundation
square up to the light to position the centre piece
correctly. Pin to hold it in position.
3. Sort out your scrap fabrics for the 'logs' into
darks and lights. Each block will need three from
each group. There is no need to keep the same
sequence of fabrics in each block. You will get
more of a 'scrap look' with a variety of fabrics.
4. Starting with a light fabric, cut a strip to cover the

first 'log' including seam allowances and place right side down against the centre square with raw edges together. Turn the foundation over and carefully holding or pinning the fabric in position, stitch on the line between the centre square and the first log. Begin and end at least two stitches beyond each seam, and fasten off each end with a backstitch. The stitching can be done by hand or machine.

5. Turn the piece over again and with a small, sharp pair of scissors trim away excess seam allowance to reduce bulk, then flip the log over and press it flat against the foundation.

6. Using the same, light fabric cut the second log and place it right side down along the second side of the centre square and the short edge of the first log. Turn the block over again and stitch on the second line. Turn it back, trim the seam, flip over the strip and press flat as before.

7. For the third and fourth logs use a dark fabric. Cut the strips to fit and continue piecing the fabrics following the numbered sequence on the diagram, sewing on the line and trimming away excess seam allowances before flipping the strip and pressing it flat against the foundation.

8. Continue adding strips keeping the light and dark sequence correct. On the final round, make sure that you have enough width on the strips to allow 1/4 in / 6 mm seam allowance beyond the outer edges for joining the blocks. Trim the calico and fabric leaving 1/4 in / 6 mm all round the outer line of the blocks.

9. Make 35 more blocks following the same sequence.

PUTTING THE BLOCKS TOGETHER

1. Using the illustration as a guide, arrange the blocks, then stitch them together through all thicknesses with a 1/4 in / 6 mm seam allowance.

2. Sew blocks together into pairs, then into larger blocks of four blocks each. Sew larger blocks into three horizontal rows.

3. Stitch horizontal rows together to complete the central section of the quilt top.

4. Press seams open as you work.

ADDING THE BORDERS

1. Piece the dark and light strips, six for each side of the quilt. Refer to the picture for the suggested colour sequence.

2. Attach corner posts to each end of two of the pieced border strips.

3. Before stitching the border strips to the quilt, back them with strips of calico to equalise the weight of the blocks and borders. See the instructions for Straight Furrow.

4. Stitch the two short borders to opposite edges of the quilt; then press.

5. Stitch on the two long borders, those with corner posts, making sure the light and dark sequence fits. Match the points at the corners.

QUILTING AND FINISHING

1. Smooth the quilt top onto the backing fabric. No wadding is required as the foundation provides enough weight.

2. Baste the quilt top to the backing in a grid.

3. Machine-quilt 'in-the-ditch' by stitching along the seams which join the blocks and across the blocks diagonally, using invisible machine quilting thread. Stitch just inside the seam which joins the borders to the central panel.

4. Finish the edges with the prepared binding strips, mitring each corner as directed in the Techniques section.

BLACK-EYED SUE

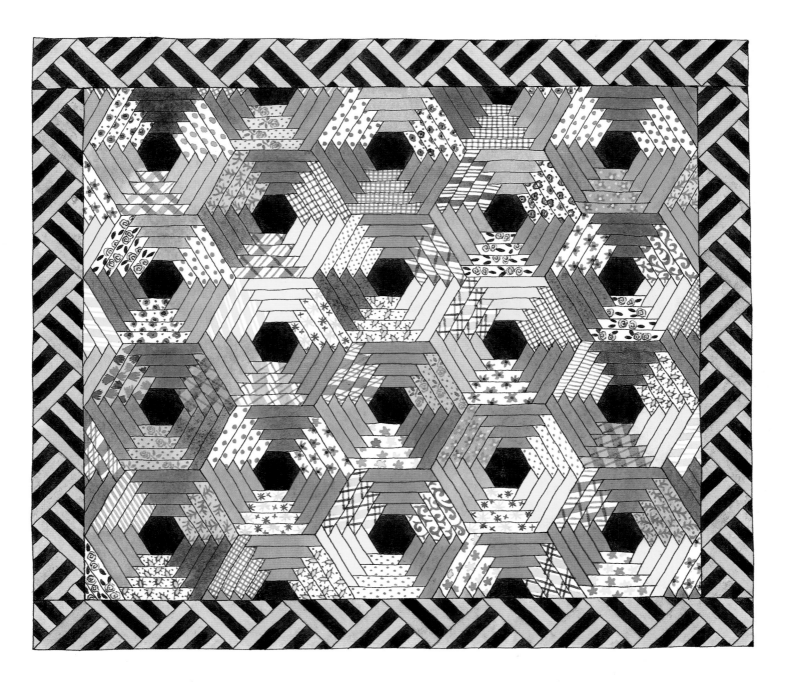

In this variation, the log cabin treatment is applied around
hexagon centres. Six sets of strips in a variety of alternating print
and solid fabrics surround each of the black hexagons.

Mennonite Joseph's Coat

B A R S

Bars is a design of quintessential simplicity - repeating parallel bands of fabric surrounded by a border. This stark design is a favourite with the Pennsylvania Amish, the large unpieced areas of solid fabrics drawing attention to the elaborate quilting designs.

The Mennonite quilt shown here, Joseph's Coat takes its name from the biblical story of Joseph and his coat of many colours. The wide bands provide an ideal vehicle to experiment with linear quilting patterns - cables, chevrons, Greek key and feather patterns are all represented here.

Skill level: Easy
Finished quilt: 70 x 78 in / 177.8 x 198.1 cm
Finished strip width: 2 in / 5.1 cm

MATERIALS

7 different solid fabrics 1 yard / metre each
Wadding 74 x 82 in / 188 x 208.2 cm
Backing / self-binding 5 yards / metres

CUTTING INSTRUCTIONS

1. For the centre panel, cut ten strips from each colour 2½ in / 6.4 cm wide across the full width of the fabric. Trim off selvedges.
2. For the pieced border, cut ten strips, 2½ x 10 in / 6.4 x 25.4 cm from each colour.

PIECING THE STRIPS

1. Working with one colour at a time, join two strips together along the short end to make five long strips in each of seven colours. Cut strips down to 61 in / 155 cm. Set aside leftover strips for the pieced border.
2. Join the strips in the desired sequence, pressing seams to one side as you work. Be careful when pressing not to allow any small pleats to form along the seam line.
3. Measure the panel and trim the sides straight. The panel should measure 60½ x 70½ in / 153.7 x 179.1 cm.

ADDING THE BORDER

1. Sew the border strips into the same colour sequence as for the centre panel, off-setting each successive strip by 2 in / 5.1 cm on the edges as you sew.

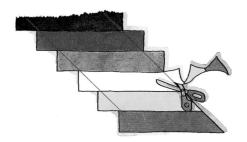

2. When you have stitched together enough strips to accommodate the length of the sides of the centre panel, cut off the projecting corners of the strips to straighten the edges. The border strips will be 5½ in / 14 cm wide.

3. To reduce fabric waste, cut the border strips in half across the middle at an angle of 90° to the sides, then reverse the pieces to join the two angled edges. Take care to keep the colour sequence correct.
4. Attach the strips to the top and bottom, then to the sides of the centre panel.

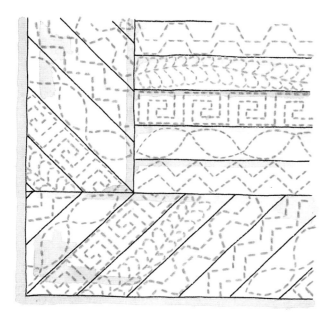

QUILTING AND FINISHING

1. Press the quilt carefully on the back and front. Remove all loose threads which may show through to the front.

2. From the selection of quilting patterns supplied, mark the individual 'bars' with cables, chevrons, Greek keys and feathers using your preferred method.

3. Assemble the three layers, making sure to centre the pieced top on the backing and wadding. Baste in a grid.

4. Quilt, working from the centre outwards.

5. When quilting is complete, finish the edges with self-binding as directed in the Techniques section.

CHINESE COINS CRIB QUILT

In this crib quilt an element of ornamentation enters into the simple equation of parallel bands. To create the Chinese Coins pattern alternate bands are randomly pieced into strips of horizontal bars. This is an ideal project if you have a collection of colourful solid scraps - no two versions of this quilt would look the same.

Skill level: Easy
Finished quilt: 32 x 47 in / 81.3 x 119.4 cm

MATERIALS

Blue for plain bars, border and binding 1¼ yards / metres

Black print ½ yard / metre

Assorted scraps of solid fabrics at least 2 x 3½ in / 5.1 x 8.9 cm to total 1 yard / metre

Wadding 35 x 50 in / 89 x 127 cm

Backing 1 yard / metre

CUTTING INSTRUCTIONS

Blue fabric

1. Cut three strips, 3½ x 36½ in / 8.9 x 92.7 cm, for the plain bars.
2. Cut two strips, 2½ x 39 in / 6.4 x 99 cm and two strips 2½ x 28 in / 6.4 x 71.1 cm, for the inner border. The remaining fabric from these strips can be used in the pieced bars.
3. Cut two strips, 2½ x 35 in / 6.4 x 89 cm and two strips, 2½ x 50 in / 6.4 x 127 cm for the binding.

Black print fabric

1. Cut two strips, 3½ x 43 in / 8.9 x 109.2 cm and two strips 3½ x 34 in / 8.9 x 86.4 cm for the outer borders. These measurements are generous to allow for trimming to fit.

Scrap fabrics

1. Cut scraps into 3½ in / 8.9 cm lengths, then into widths of between 1½ - 2½ in / 3.8 - 6.4 cm for the bars.

PIECING THE PATCHWORK BARS

1. Piece together the assorted 3½ in / 8.9 cm strips placing widths and colours randomly. Make three sets of strips, each 36½ in / 92.7 cm long. If necessary trim a fraction off the end of the top or bottom strip to adjust the size.
2. Sew the pieced and plain bars together using the picture as a guide.

ADDING THE BORDERS

1. Stitch the two longer blue inner border strips to the top and bottom of the bars panel; trim edges to fit.
2. Stitch the two shorter inner border strips to the remaining sides, trimming again as necessary.
3. Repeat with the black print border strips.

QUILTING AND FINISHING

1. If you are using 44 in / 111.8 cm fabric for the backing, the length of the quilt top will be just over the width of fabric. Rather than buy double the length of backing, insert a pieced panel to extend the size of the backing. Cut the backing fabric in half down the length of the fabric; remove selvedges and piece in a 'bars' panel with strips cut 1½ - 2½ x 5½ in / 3.8 - 6.4 x 14 cm.

2. The quilting design is a diagonal grid worked in straight line. These can be marked as you work with ¼ in / 6 mm masking tape, or measured by eye.
3. Assemble the quilt and baste the three layers together.
4. Quilt, working from the centre outwards.
5. When quilting is complete, fold the binding strips in half and apply as directed for straight binding in the Techniques section.

DIAMOND BARS

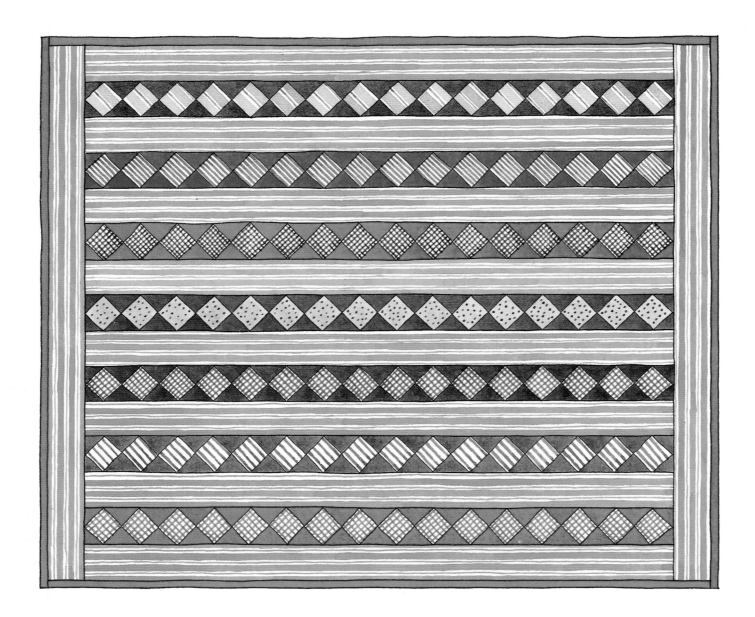

Pink, candy-striped strips alternating with pieced strips
made up of diamond shapes give this variation its light-hearted appeal.

Skill level: Intermediate
Finished quilt: 64 x 77 in / 162.6 x 195.6 cm
Finished square: 3 x 3 in / 7.6 x 7.6 cm

MATERIALS

Pink candy stripes for bars and backing 5 yards / metres

Seven solid and seven contrasting print fabrics for the diamond bars 1/4 yard / metre each

Red for binding 1/2 yard / metre

Wadding 70 x 82 in / 177.8 x 208.2 cm

CUTTING INSTRUCTIONS

Pink candy-stripe fabric

1. Cut eight strips, 4³/4 x 72 in / 12 x 182.9 cm, and two strips, 4³/4 x 68 in / 12 x 172.7 cm. These measurements are generous so that you can trim to fit. Reserve the rest for the backing.

Assorted solid and print fabrics

1. Cut 16 squares, 3¹/2 x 3¹/2 in / 8.9 x 8.9 cm from each print fabric for the diamonds.

2. From each solid fabric, cut 8 squares 5¹/2 x 5¹/2 in / 14 x 14 cm for the side triangles. Divide each of these into four by cutting across both diagonals.

3. Cut two squares 3 x 3 in / 7.6 x 7.6 cm. Cut diagonally in half to make four corner triangles.

Red fabric

1. Cut strips 2¹/2 in / 6.4 cm wide, joining as necessary for the binding.

PIECING THE DIAMOND BARS

1. Join a side triangle to each side of 14 squares.

2. Join two corner triangles and one side triangle to the remaining two squares for the ends of the rows.

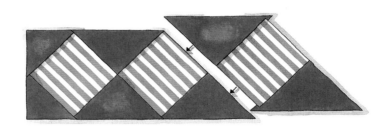

3. Now join the diamond units together matching points.

4. Make up seven pieced bars.

JOINING THE BARS

1. Arrange the bars in the desired order and join each to one of the longer strips of the candy-striped fabric. Trim the length on the striped fabric to fit the pieced bars.

2. Refer to the illustration and join pieces so striped and pieced bars alternate, finishing with a candy-striped bar on the top and bottom of the panel.

3. Add the two shorter candy-striped strips to the sides of the panel, trimming to fit.

QUILTING AND FINISHING

1. Give the quilt a final press on the back and front and trim off any loose threads.

2. If you plan to use an elaborate quilting design such as a running cable or feather on the striped bars, mark this on before layering. Use the templates provided for the Joseph's Coat quilt. Straight line quilting such as contour or grid quilting can be marked as you work with 1/4 in / 6 mm masking tape, or measured by eye.

3. Assemble the three quilt layers and baste in a grid.

4. Quilt, working from the centre outwards.

5. When quilting is complete, finish the edges with a straight binding as directed in the Techniques section.

CLIMBING ROSES

This variation introduces a simple appliqué rose garland.
Experiment with paper cut-outs to make the flower and leaf templates.
Mark the position of the curve for the stem on the cream background
material first, then fit the appliqué along the length. Add final details
with embroidery stitches.

Amish Sunshine and Shadow

SUNSHINE AND SHADOW

Sunshine and Shadow gets its name from the concentric bands of alternating light and dark fabrics that make up the design. It is simply pieced, consisting of many rows of small squares. Similar designs, Trip Around The World, Philadelphia Pavement and Railroad are all constructed using different configurations of the one-patch, and demonstrate the versatility of such a simple component.

Skill level: Easy
Finished quilt: 38 x 38 in / 96.5 x 96.5 cm
Finished squares: 1¹/₂ in / 3.8 cm

MATERIALS

If you would like to use your own colour scheme for this simple design, draw out a plan on graph paper and note the position of each fabric within the pattern. When choosing fabrics, keep in mind that the largest number of squares in any one colour is 36, although you can use the same colour in more than one position. Each ¹/₄ yard / metre fabric piece will yield 48 squares, 2 x 2 in / 5.1 x 5.1 cm.

12 different solid fabrics for centre panel and corner squares ¹/₄ yard / metre each
Purple for inner border ¹/₄ yard / metre
Navy blue for outer border ³/₄ yard / metre
Wadding 41 x 41 in / 104 x 104 cm
Backing / binding 44 x 44 in / 111.7 x 111.7 cm

CUTTING INSTRUCTIONS

1. For individual piecing, cut the following number of 2 in / 5.1 cm squares from each fabric: 32 Pink; 12 Mauve; 32 Pale pink; 32 Black; 20 Navy Blue; 28 Green; 28 Light green; 20 Purple; 13 Bright blue; 8 Mid-blue; 4 Pale blue.

Note: If you wish to adapt these instructions to use the quick strip-piecing method, cut two strips, 2 in / 5.1 cm wide across the full width of each required fabric. Sew strips together in sequence to make a pieced strip, as illustrated in the 'Mosaic Tiles' variation. Cut pieced strips apart at 1¹/₄ in / 3.8 cm intervals, and sew together around a centre square to produce the pattern.

2. From the purple fabric, cut four strips 2 x 23 in / 5.1 x 58.4 cm for the inner border.
3. From the navy blue fabric, cut four strips 6¹/₂ x 26 in / 16.5 x 66 cm for the outer border.
4. Cut four squares, 6¹/₂ x 6¹/₂ in / 16.5 x 16.5 cm from the dark green fabric for the large corner posts.

CONSTRUCTING THE CENTRE PANEL

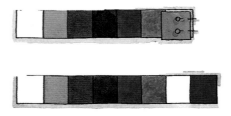

1. Sew the squares together in sequence to form pieced strips working from the centre square outwards.

2. Press seam allowances in adjacent rows in alternate directions. Sew the rows together in the correct sequence, locking opposing seam allowances to match points.

3. Press well on the back and front.

ADDING THE BORDERS

1. Stitch two of the inner borders to either side of the centre panel.

2. Stitch green corner posts to each short side of the remaining inner border strips before attaching these to the top and bottom of the central panel.

3. Repeat this sequence using the wide outer borders and the 6$\frac{1}{2}$ in / 16.5 cm corner posts.

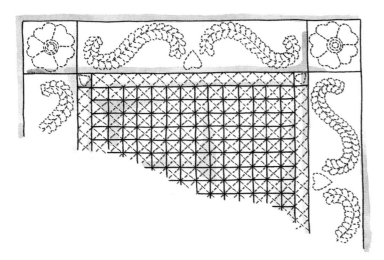

QUILTING AND FINISHING

1. Give the quilt top a final press and trim away any loose threads on the back.

2. From the templates supplied, mark quilting patterns onto the borders. The centre panel is quilted in straight line and can be marked with $\frac{1}{4}$ in / 6 mm masking tape.

3. Assemble the quilt layers, making sure that you position the quilt top centrally, leaving enough of the backing to extend beyond the top for self-binding.

4. Baste in a grid working outwards from the centre.

5. Quilt from the centre outwards, finishing with the feather and heart designs on the outer borders.

6. When quilting is complete trim the wadding even with the quilt top. Trim away excess backing to leave a 1 in / 2.5 cm border all around.

7. Bring the backing over to the front of the quilt with a double fold. Slipstitch the fold to the right side of the quilt, mitring each corner as instructed in the Techniques section.

PHILADELPHIA PAVEMENT

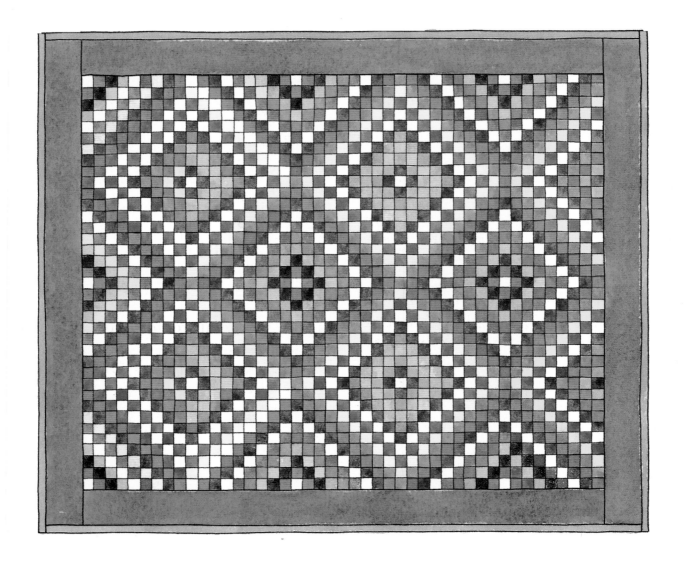

The Philadelphia Pavement design uses multiple versions of the
Sunshine and Shadow pattern. It is a maze of bright, solid colours linked by
a network of diagonal red squares. Colour variations within the blocks blend and
match, together forming a complex design which is harnessed by the border.

Skill level: Easy
Finished quilt: 86 x 104 in / 218.4 x 264.2 cm
Finished block: 18 x 18 in / 45.7 x 45.7 cm
Number of blocks: 20

MATERIALS

Red 1 yard / metre

12 assorted solid fabrics each ¼ - ½ yard / metre depending on placement

    (¼ yard / metre will yield 42 squares)

Green for border 1¾ yards / metres

Wadding 89 x 107 in / 226.1 x 271.8 cm

Backing 6 yards / metres

Binding ¾ yards / metres

CUTTING INSTRUCTIONS

1. Cut approximately 220 squares, 2½ x 2½ in / 6.4 x 6.4 cm from the red fabric. Depending on placement, you may need to cut more.

2. Referring to the illustration or your own chart, cut the requisite number of 2½ in / 6.4 cm squares from each fabric. Keep in mind that you must be able to repeat four blocks for the pattern to work.

3. Cut eight border strips, 6½ in / 16.5 cm wide across the full width of the green fabric. Join as necessary to make two strips, 76 in / 193 cm and two strips, 94 in / 238.7 cm.

4. For the binding, cut nine strips, 2½ in / 6.4 cm wide across the full width of the fabric. Join strips as necessary.

CONSTRUCTING THE CENTRE PANEL

1. Stitch the squares together in blocks, nine by nine, so that the red squares form diagonal line which will link with adjoining blocks to form diamonds. Using the picture as a guide, note that on some of the blocks, the red squares will be one row away from the diagonal, to keep the step sequence correct.

2. One extra row of squares is needed along the top of the quilt. Add this row to the appropriate blocks.

3. When all the blocks are constructed, sew them together matching seams and pressing as you work.

4. Stitch the longer borders to the top and bottom of the quilt. Trim the ends even with the central panel. Press.

5. Add the longer borders to either side, trimming once again.

QUILTING AND FINISHING

1. Press the quilt top carefully. Trim away any loose threads.

2. Mark the quilt top if you plan to use a specific quilting pattern.

3. Assemble the quilt layers and baste in a grid.

4. Quilt in the desired pattern starting at the centre and working out toward the borders. Contour quilting or quilting in a diamond grid can be marked as you work with ¼ in / 6 mm masking tape.

5. When quilting is complete, apply the prepared binding to the edges of the quilt as directed for separate binding in the Techniques section.

MOSAIC TILES

Mosaic Tiles is made of large blocks with 1 in / 2.5 cm squares cut from tiny scraps of fabric and set on point. These alternate with larger squares of fabric which provide an area to display your quilting skills. The design has been updated with a quick strip-piecing method.

Skill level: Intermediate
Finished quilt: 50 x 78 in / 127 x 198 cm
Finished block: 14 x 14 in / 35.6 x 35.6 cm
Number of blocks: 7

MATERIALS

11 assorted fabrics each ⅛ yard / metre
Solid blue fabric for the plain squares, border and
binding 2½ yards / metres
Wadding 53 x 81 in / 134.6 x 205.7 cm
Backing 3 yards / metres

CUTTING INSTRUCTIONS

Assorted fabrics

1. From each of the eleven fabrics, cut two strips,
1½ in / 3.8 cm wide across the full width of the
fabric. If you are using scraps, cut 1½ in / 3.8 cm
wide strips and sew together to make a total length
of 66 in / 167.6 cm.

Blue fabric

1. Cut eight squares, 14½ x 14½ in / 36.8 x 36.8
cm for the plain setting squares.
2. For the borders, cut six strips 4½ in / 11.4 cm
across the full width of the fabric.
3. For the binding, cut six strips, 2½ in / 6.4 cm
wide across the full width of the fabric.

PIECING THE BLOCK

Note: It is very important to use an accurate ¼ in /
6 mm seam allowance when piecing these blocks.
Also, set the stitch length on your sewing machine
to 10-12 stitches per 1 in / 2.5 cm.

1. For each block, arrange the strips in the desired
sequence trying out different versions before
making a final decision.
2. When you are happy with the result, pin and
sew the strips right sides together.
3. Once you have sewn all eleven strips together,
press the seams in alternate directions from the

back, making sure there are no pleats or puckers
on the front. Then press carefully on the right side.

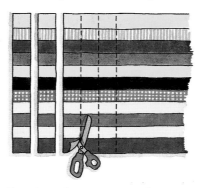

4. Use a quilter's ruler to straighten one end of the
pieced strip by trimming the end at a 90° angle to the
seams. Now cut the pieced strip at 1½ in / 3.8 cm
intervals to make 44 bands.
5. Each block is constructed in four quarters. Begin
with one section and work outwards from the
centre to the right-hand side. The centre row uses
all 11 fabrics: take one of the cut bands and place
on a flat surface with fabric number 11 at the top.
6. Take a second band and unpick fabric number 1
from the bottom. Pin the bands together so that
they are off-set or stepped by one square. Sew the
seam, locking the opposing seam allowances to
match points.

7. For the third row, unpick two squares (fabrics 1
and 2). Drop the band by another square at the top
and sew the seam as before.

8. Continue removing squares from the bottom, increasing the number removed by one on each subsequent band until you have joined ten rows.

9. To complete the first quarter, sew a 1½ in / 3.8 cm square of fabric number 11 to the corner. Note that this square will form the side and corner triangles of the block.

10. Work the remaining quarters in the same way, keeping the sequence of fabrics correct and discarding the unpicked squares.

11. When all four quarters have been sewn, use your quilter's rule to trim away the outside corners. The red pencil line in the illustration is your sewing line, so remember to leave a ¼ in / 6 mm seam allowance beyond this marking for joining to the plain blue setting squares.

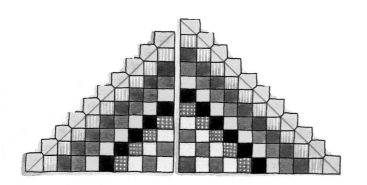

12. Join the four quarters to complete the block, taking care to match points.

13. Make six more pieced blocks following the same sequence.

14. Measure each pieced block to ensure they are perfect 14½ in / 36.8 cm squares. If they vary in size, you will need to ease them to fit the setting squares.

PUTTING THE BLOCKS TOGETHER

1. Sew the blocks together in three horizontal rows of five blocks each, alternating plain and pieced blocks, easing to fit where necessary. Press carefully.

2. Sew the rows together, taking care to match points between blocks. Press.

ADDING THE BORDER

1. Join the border strips to make up two lengths, 54 in / 137.2 cm, and two lengths 74 in / 188 cm. Stitch the longer border strips to the top and bottom of the quilt. Press borders out. Trim away excess.

2. Now stitch the remaining border strips to the sides. Press out, then trim the ends even.

QUILTING AND FINISHING

1. Cut the backing in half and stitch with a ½ in / 1.3 cm seam along the selvedges. Trim off the selvedges. Press.

2. Press the quilt top carefully, trimming away any loose threads which may show through to the front.

3. From the quilting patterns supplied, transfer your design to the plain blocks and borders.

4. Assemble the three layers and baste together in a grid.

5. Quilt in the desired pattern, working from the centre out towards the border.

6. When you have finished quilting, bind the edges with the prepared binding strips as directed for straight binding in the Techniques section.

RAILROAD CROSSING

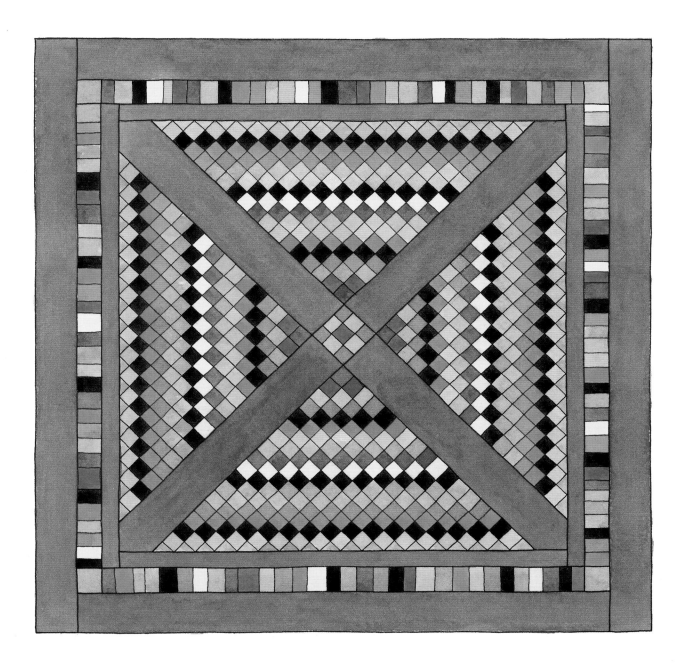

The centre panel of the quilt can be constructed in four triangular-shaped quarters; a section of the sashing is stitched along one side of each triangle before being joined to a nine-patch at the centre.

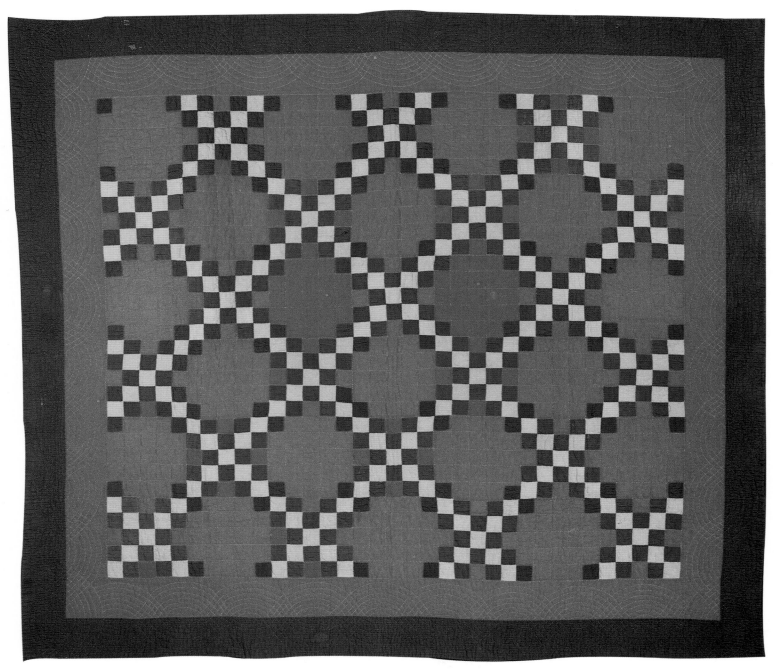

Mennonite Double Irish Chain

IRISH CHAIN

The Irish Chain patterns are all formed from a combination of two blocks of differing complexity. The two blocks which make up the Double Irish Chain interlink ingeniously giving a seemingly complex design with strong diagonal emphasis. Made here in bold primary colours of red, blue and yellow the quilt makes a dramatic statement.

Skill level: Easy
Finished quilt: 82 x 92 in / 208.3 x 233.7 cm
Finished block: 10 x 10 in / 25.4 x 25.4 cm
Number of blocks: 42

MATERIALS

Red 3¼ yards / metres
Blue 2¾ yards / metres
Yellow 1 yard / metre
Backing 5½ yards / metres
Wadding 86 x 96 in / 218.4 x 243.8 cm

CUTTING INSTRUCTIONS

All the pieces for the blocks can be cut without templates using the rotary cutting method. However, if preferred, templates can be made for hand or machine piecing. Seam allowances are included in the measurements given so if you are making templates bear this in mind. When cutting border and binding strips, remember 3 - 4 in / 7.6 - 10.2 cm have been added to the finished length to allow for adjustment.

Red fabric

1. For the inner borders, cut two strips, 6 x 72 in / 15.2 x 187.9 cm and two strips, 6 x 74 in / 15.2 x 187.9 cm.
2. For Block 1, cut 84 B rectangles, 2½ x 6½ in / 6.4 x 16.5 cm and 21 C squares, 6½ x 6½ in / 16.5 x 16.5 cm.

Blue fabric

1. For the outer borders, cut two strips, 6 x 83 in / 15.2 x 210.8 cm and two strips, 6 x 84 in / 15.2 x 213.4 cm.
2. For the binding, cut two strips, 2½ x 85 in / 6.4 x 215.9 cm and two strips, 2½ x 93 in / 6.4 x 236.2 cm.
3. For Block 1, cut 84 A squares, 2½ x 2½ in / 6.4 x 6.4 cm. For Block 2, cut 252 A squares, 2½ x 2½ in / 6.4 x 6.4 cm.

Yellow fabric

1. For Block 2, cut 189 A squares, 2½ x 2½ in / 6.4 x 6.4 cm.

PIECING THE BLOCKS

Block 1

1. Sew a B rectangle to each side of a C square. Press.
2. Sew two blue A squares to each short end of remaining B rectangles. Press.
3. Sew the two seams to join the ABA units to the BCB unit, matching points.

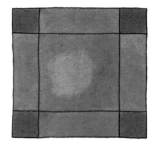

Block 2

1. Sew A squares together into five strips in the colour sequence illustrated. Press seam allowances of rows in alternate directions.
2. Sew the strips together matching seams.

PUTTING THE BLOCKS TOGETHER

1. Make a total of 21 blocks in each design.

2. Sew blocks into six rows of seven blocks each, alternating the block designs. In the top right-hand corner, a blue square has been exchanged for a red one which makes this block seem to merge with the inner red border.

ADDING THE BORDERS

1. Sew the shorter red borders to opposite sides of the quilt. Press, then sew the longer red borders to the top and bottom.

2. Sew the blue outer borders to the quilt following the same sequence.

QUILTING AND FINISHING

1. Give the quilt top a final press on the back and front. Trim away any loose threads which may show through to the front.

2. Mark the cable quilting pattern supplied on either side of the border seams using your preferred method. Add a further five rings to fill a 5½ in / 14 cm finished border. The central section will be quilted in-the-ditch which can be done by eye or marked with ¼ in / 6 mm masking tape as you work.

3. Assemble the quilt layers and baste in a grid.

4. Quilt the pieced blocks from the centre outwards and extend the lines which follow the pattern across the large red areas of each Block 1 to form a cross-hatch design.

5. Quilt the cable pattern across the two border fabrics. Use cream quilting thread, so that your stitches blend with some of the fabrics and contrast with others such as the dark, outer border.

6. When quilting is complete, bind the raw edges of the quilt with the prepared binding strips as instructed for straight binding.

SINGLE IRISH CHAIN

The Single Irish Chain, the most easily attainable pattern for a beginner, is here given a cool crispness with a cream and blue colour scheme. A quality of movement results by setting the simple nine-patch blocks on point, and the alternate plain cream squares seen here as diamonds provide a fine area to display quilting skills.

Skill level: Easy
Finished quilt: 57 x 70 in / 144.8 x 177.8 cm
Finished block: 9 x 9 in / 22.9 x 22.9 cm
Number of blocks: 20

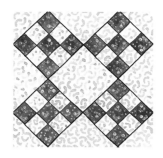

MATERIALS

Blue fabric 2¼ yards / metres
White fabric 2½ yards / metres
Backing 4 yards / metres
Wadding 65 x 74 in / 165.1 x 188 cm

CUTTING INSTRUCTIONS

White fabric
1. Cut four squares, 14 x 14 in / 35.6 x 35.6 cm. Cut across both diagonals of three squares to make 12 triangles. Then using one triangle as a template, cut two more triangles from the fourth square for a total of 14 side triangles.
2. For the corner triangles, cut four right-angle triangles with 7¼ in / 18.4 cm sides from the remaining fabric left over from cutting the side triangles.
3. Cut 12 setting squares, 9½ x 9½ in / 24.1 x 24.1 cm.
4. For the blocks, cut six strips, 3½ in / 8.9 cm wide, across the width of the fabric.
5. Cut binding strips 2½ in / 6.4 cm wide and join to make a continuous length.

Blue fabric
1. Cut two border strips, 3½ x 67 in / 8.9 x 170.1 cm and two border strips, 3½ x 62 in / 8.9 x 157.5 cm. This allows enough for trimming to size when the borders are sewn to the quilt.
2. Cut six strips, 3½ in / 8.9 cm wide, across the

width of the fabric. If strips are of uneven length, make a join in the shorter strips to equalise the lengths. Cut out the join as you construct the blocks.

PIECING THE BLOCKS

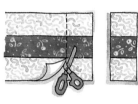

1. Stitch the strips together in the following two sequences: blue / white / blue and white / blue / white. Press seams towards the blue fabric. You will need twice as many of the blue / white / blue sequence.

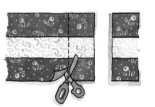

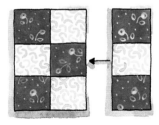

2. Cut the pieced strips at 3½ in / 8.9 cm intervals. Pin, then sew strips together to form the nine-patch block, locking opposing seams to match points.

3. Make a total of 20 blocks, cutting and stitching more strip sets as required.

PUTTING THE QUILT TOP TOGETHER

1. Arrange the nine-patch blocks alternately with the white setting squares.
2. Place the side and corner triangles in position at each end of the diagonal rows of blocks. Pin, then stitch the blocks together in diagonal rows making sure that the correct triangles are at each end. Press seams towards the nine-patch blocks.

3. Stitch the rows together in the correct order matching seams.

4. Add top left and bottom right-hand corner squares last.

5. Add the border strips, first to the top and bottom, then to the sides, trimming even with the pieced top as appropriate. If preferred, finish the corners of the border with a mitre as directed in the Techniques section.

QUILTING AND FINISHING

1. Give the quilt top a final press on the back and front. Trim away any loose threads which may show through to the front.

2. Mark the feathered circle quilting motif to the setting squares, using your preferred method.

3. Assemble the quilt layers and baste in a grid.

4. Quilt, working from the centre outwards.

5. Prepare the binding strips and apply as directed in the Techniques section for continuous binding.

TRIPLE IRISH CHAIN

The Triple Irish Chain is the most complex of the Irish Chain designs.
Here a chequerboard of red and white squares creates a kinetic effect while
the secondary blocks in a harmonising red print, anchor the design.

Skill level: Moderate
Finished quilt: 76 x 95¼ in / 193 x 241.9 cm
Finished block: 13½ x 13½ in / 34.3 x 34.3 cm
Number of blocks: 32

MATERIALS

Dark fabric 5¼ yards / metres
Light fabric 2½ yards / metres
Backing / binding 5½ yards / metres
Wadding 80 x 100 in / 203.2 x 254 cm

CUTTING INSTRUCTIONS

Dark fabric

1. For the side triangles, cut four squares 20³/₈ x 20³/₈ in / 51.8 x 51.8 cm. Divide three into quarter-square triangles, then cut two more from the fourth square.
2. The corner triangles can be cut from the remaining fabric left over from cutting the side triangles. Cut four right-angle triangles with 10½ in / 26.7 cm sides.
3. Refer to the diagram of the two blocks. Cut 24 B rectangles, 3½ x 8 in / 8.9 x 20.3 cm and 12 C rectangles, 8 x 14 in / 20.3 x 35.6 cm.
4. Cut 23 strips, 2 in / 5.1 cm wide across the full width of the fabric. Set five strips aside for Block 1 and 18 strips aside for Block 2.

Light fabric

1. Cut 23 strips, 2 in / 5.1 cm wide across the full width of the fabric. Five strips will be used for Block 1, and 18 strips for Block 2.

PIECING THE BLOCKS

Block 1

1. Using an exact ¼ in / 6 mm seam allowance, sew dark and light strips together, alternating colours, to make five pairs. Press seams towards the darker strip.

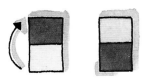

2. Cut across the strips at 2 in / 5.1 cm intervals. Take two sections and reverse one to make the four-patch for the corner of Block 1. Lock opposing seams and stitch together.

3. Sew a total of 48 four-patch blocks.

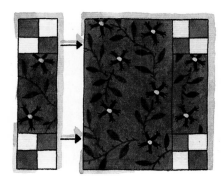

4. Stitch a four-patch block to each short side of a B rectangle being careful to position the dark / light squares correctly for each block. Repeat.

5. Join these units to each long side of a C rectangle.

6. Make a total of 12 blocks.

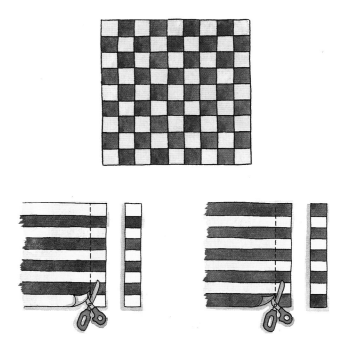

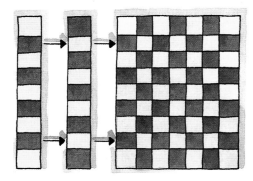

Block 2

1. Stitch the remaining 2 in / 5.1 cm strips together in two sets of nine. Make one set with light fabric on the outer edges and one set with dark. Press seams towards the dark fabric.

2. Cut across the strips at 2 in / 5.1 cm intervals and make up the blocks by stitching alternate sections together in sets of nine, locking opposing seams to match points.

3. Make 20 blocks in total, cutting more strips as required.

PUTTING THE BLOCKS TOGETHER

1. Arrange the blocks alternately as illustrated. Place side and corner triangles in position at each end of the diagonal rows.

2. Pin, then stitch the blocks together into diagonal rows. Press seams towards each Block 1.

3. Stitch the rows together in the correct order, matching seams.

4. Finally, add the top left and bottom right corner triangles.

QUILTING AND FINISHING

1. Give the quilt top a final press on the back and front. Trim away any loose threads which may show through to the front.

2. Mark the plain areas of each Block 1 with your chosen quilting pattern. If you wish to quilt in straight line (contour or diamond grid), this can be marked as you work with 1/4 in / 6 mm masking tape.

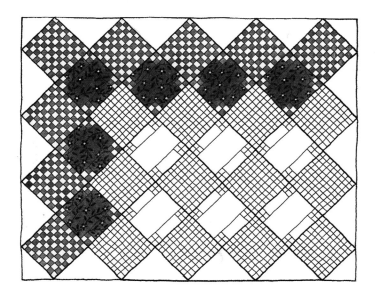

3. Cut the backing fabric into two equal lengths. Cut off selvedges, then seam together down the longer sides.

4. If you are using straight binding, cut two strips, 2¹/₂ in / 6.4 cm wide, down the length of each side of the joined backing.

5. Assemble the three layers of the quilt and baste in a grid.

6. Quilt, working from the centre outwards.

7. When quilting is complete, finish the raw edges of the quilt with either separate or self-binding.

PUMPKIN PATCH

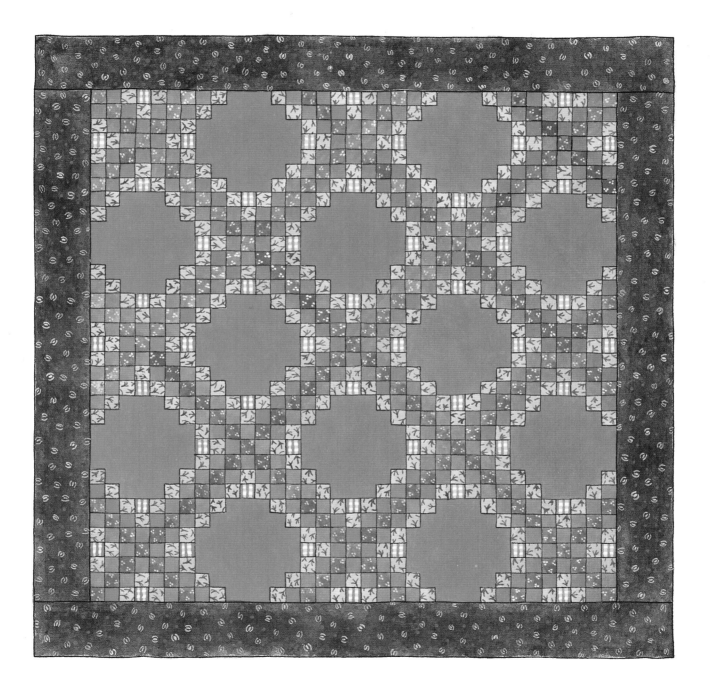

The third variation uses a striking combination of red, blue and
yellow for the blocks offset by a brown print border.

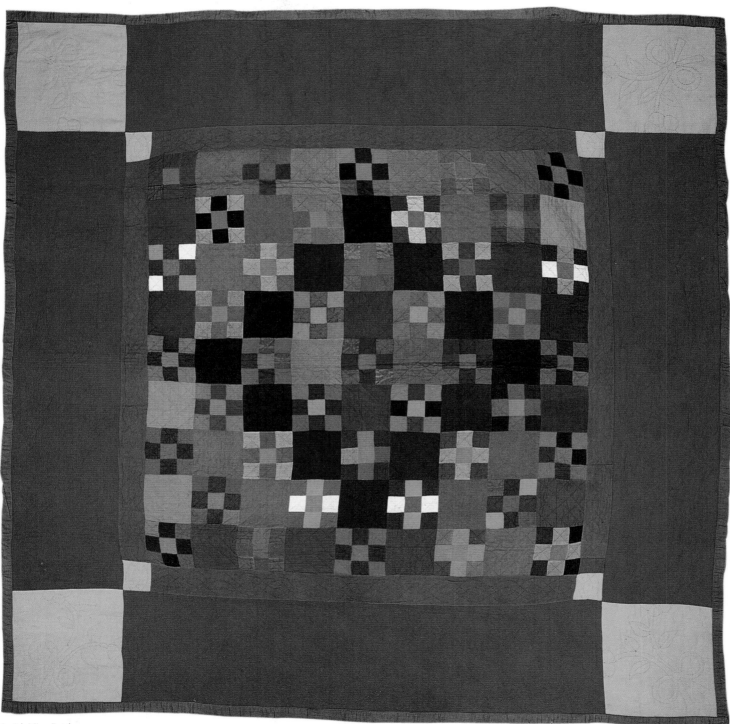

Amish Nine-Patch

NINE-PATCH

The nine-patch block - nine squares stitched together
in a three by three grid - is one of the simplest quilt blocks.

The seemingly random placement of bright, solid colours in this quilt
is given structure with the diamond of black squares. Some blocks are
composed of just two colours, others of three and some have more.
It would make a more challenging project to use the quilt as an
inspiration rather than make a direct copy and create a colour palette
which is essentially your own. Some blocks are made of colours and
values which contrast highly while others use fabrics which seem to
merge together. Note the use of light coloured squares, used
selectively to highlight certain areas of the quilt.

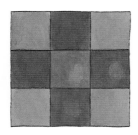

Skill level: Easy
Finished quilt: 83 x 83 in / 210.8 x 210.8 cm
Finished block: 6³/4 x 6³/4 in / 17.1 x 17.1 cm
Number of blocks: 41

MATERIALS

Black ³/4 yard / metre
Assorted colours totalling 1¹/2 yards / metres for
setting squares
  (¹/4 yard / metre will yield five squares)
Assorted colours totalling 3³/4 yards / metres for
the nine-patch blocks
  (¹/4 yard / metre will yield 24 squares)
Green for inner border ³/4 yard / metre
Purple for outer border 2 yards / metres
Turquoise for corner posts ¹/4 yard / metre
Wadding 88 x 88 in / 223.5 x 223.5 cm
Backing 5 yards / metres
Binding ³/4 yard / metre

CUTTING INSTRUCTIONS

Assorted fabrics
1. Cut 369 squares, 2³/4 x 2³/4 in / 7 x 7 cm, for the
nine-patch blocks.
2. Cut 28 setting squares, 7¹/4 x 7¹/4 in / 18.4 x
18.4 cm in a wide variety of colours.

Black fabric
1. Cut 12 setting squares, 7¹/4 x 7¹/4 in / 18.4 x
18.4 cm.

Green fabric
1. Cut four strips, 3¹/2 x 65 in / 8.9 x 165 cm, for
the inner border.
2. Cut four strips, 2¹/2 x 86 in / 6.4 x 218.4 cm, for
the binding strips, joining if necessary.

Turquoise fabric
1. Cut four squares 3¹/2 x 3¹/2 in / 8.9 x 8.9 cm, for
the inner corner posts.
2. Cut four squares, 8¹/2 x 8¹/2 in / 21.6 x 21.6 cm,
for the outer corner posts.

Purple fabric
1. Cut four strips, 8¹/2 x 71 in / 21.6 x 180.3 cm,
for the outer borders. Extra length has been
allowed for trimming to fit.

PIECING THE BLOCKS

1. For each block,
arrange the squares on
a flat surface, in the
colour arrangement of
your choice, then
stitch three rows of
three squares each. On
the centre row, press
seams away from the
centre square; on the
two outer rows, press
seams towards the
centre so that points
can be matched by
locking opposing seam
allowances.

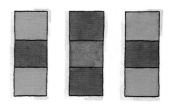

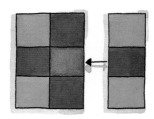

2. Make a total of 41 nine-patch blocks.

PUTTING THE BLOCKS TOGETHER

1. Alternate the pieced nine-patch blocks and plain setting squares making sure the position of the black squares forms a diamond.
2. Pin, then sew the plain and pieced blocks together into nine double nine-patch blocks. Stitch three rows of three double nine-patch blocks each.
3. Finally, sew the three rows of blocks together. Press. The sides should measure 61$\frac{1}{4}$ x 61$\frac{1}{4}$ in / 155.6 x 155.6 cm.

ADDING THE BORDERS

1. Pin, then stitch two of the inner border strips to opposite sides of the quilt. Press, then trim away excess.
2. Stitch two small corner posts to each short end of the remaining inner border strips, and stitch these to the top and bottom of the quilt. Press.

3. Repeat the same sequence with the outer border strips and large corner posts.

QUILTING AND FINISHING

1. From the quilting patterns supplied, mark the inner borders with a cable, outer borders with a running feather, and the large corner posts with a bouquet and bow. The straight line quilting on the centre panel of the quilt can be marked as you work with $\frac{1}{4}$ in / 6 mm masking tape or measured by eye.
2. Assemble the quilt layers and baste in a grid.
3. Quilt the top, working from the centre outwards towards the borders.
4. When quilting is complete, apply the prepared binding strips to the edges of the quilt, as directed for separate binding in the Techniques section.

SCRAP NINE-PATCH

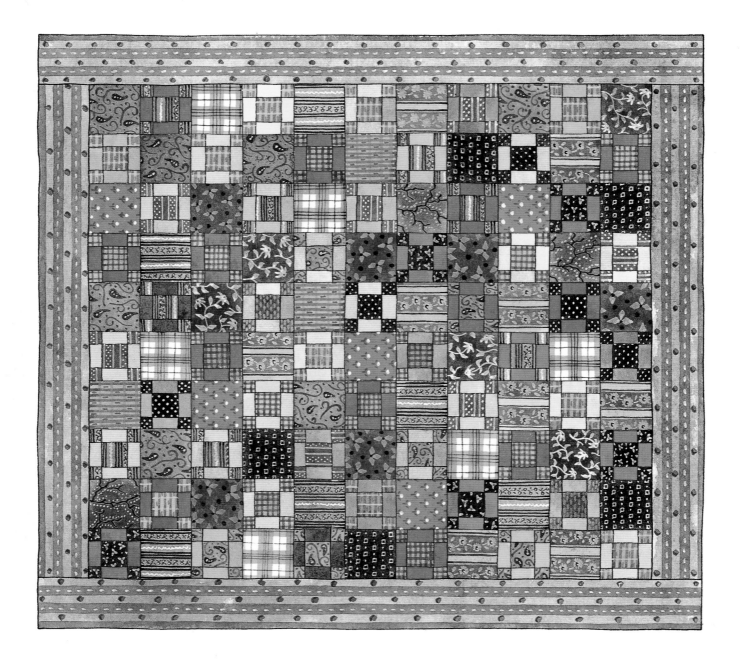

The proportions of the nine-patch are altered in this variation to give the impression of an elongated block. As in the first quilt, each nine-patch block alternates with an unpieced setting square. If you want to bring a quality of antique-quilt nostalgia, combine chintz prints with plaids and stripes in a sepia palette.

Skill level: Easy
Finished quilt: 96 x 104 in / 243.8 x 264.2 cm
Finished block: 8 x 8 in / 20.3 x 20.3 cm
Number of blocks: 55

MATERIALS

Many different fabrics are used to construct the pieced blocks and the larger setting squares. To make fabric selection easier, yardage requirements are broken down into amounts required for the pieced blocks and setting squares and, in parenthesis, the number of patches which can be cut from 1/4 yard / metre of fabric.

Assorted prints for setting squares 3 1/2 yards / metres (1/4 yard / metre will yield four)
Assorted prints for blocks 3 yards / metre (1/4 yard / metre will yield 42 A or 9 C squares)
Complementary prints for blocks 2 yards / metres (1/4 yard / metre will yield 16 B rectangles)
Striped border fabric 3 yards / metres
Wadding 100 x 108 in / 254 x 274.3 cm
Backing / binding 8 1/4 yards / metres

CUTTING INSTRUCTIONS

When constructing a scrap quilt like this, it is advisable to cut the pieces for the blocks as you make them up, deciding which fabrics to put together as you work. In most of the blocks, the A and C squares are cut from the same fabric, in some they are different but in all the blocks there is contrast in value (light / dark) between the A/C pieces and the B pieces.

For each of 55 blocks:
1. Cut four A squares, 2 1/2 x 2 1/2 in / 6.4 x 6.4 cm and one C square, 4 1/2 x 4 1/2 in / 11.4 x 11.4 cm from a printed fabric.
2. From a contrasting fabric, cut four B rectangles, 2 1/2 x 4 1/2 in / 6.4 x 11.4 cm.

1. From the assortment of printed fabrics, cut 55 setting squares, 8 1/2 x 8 1/2 in / 21.6 x 21.6 cm.
2. Cut two strips, 8 1/2 x 88 1/2 in / 21.6 x 224.8 cm, and two strips, 8 1/2 x 104 in / 21.6 x 264.2 cm for the borders.
3. Cut the backing fabric into three equal lengths, 99 in / 251.5 cm long.
4. For the binding, cut five strips, 2 1/2 in / 6.4 cm wide, from the excess backing fabric down the lengthwise grain, once you have seamed the backing.

PIECING THE BLOCKS

1. Piece three strips, ABA, BCB and ABA and join to form a block. Press seams in opposite directions.
2. Pin, then sew strips together taking care to match points.
3. Make 54 more blocks in the same way.

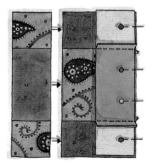

PUTTING THE BLOCKS TOGETHER

1. Alternate the setting blocks with the pieced blocks.

2. Pin, then sew blocks together, making four quarter sections first, then sewing the quarters into halves, then the two halves together. This avoids sewing all but one very long seam, along which any inaccuracies in the size of the blocks may become exaggerated. By sewing shorter seams where possible they can be eased if necessary.

3. Press the centre section of the quilt carefully once the four quarters have been joined.

ADDING THE BORDERS

1. Stitch the shorter borders to opposite sides of the quilt. Trim the ends even with the central panel. Press.

2. Stitch the longer borders to the top and bottom of the quilt, trimming once again. Press.

QUILTING AND FINISHING

1. Seam the lengths of backing fabric together using a $1/2$ in / 1.3 cm seam allowance. Remove the selvedges and press carefully.

2. Mark the quilt top with the quilting pattern of choice, but for a quilt using such a variety of fabrics, outline quilting or a cross-hatch design is advisable. Straight line for quilting can be marked as you work with $1/4$ in / 6 mm masking tape or measured by eye.

3. Assemble the quilt layers and baste in a grid.

4. Quilt from the centre outwards.

5. When quilting is complete, join the binding strips as necessary to make a continuous straight binding. Fold and apply separate binding as directed in the Techniques section.

DOUBLE NINE-PATCH

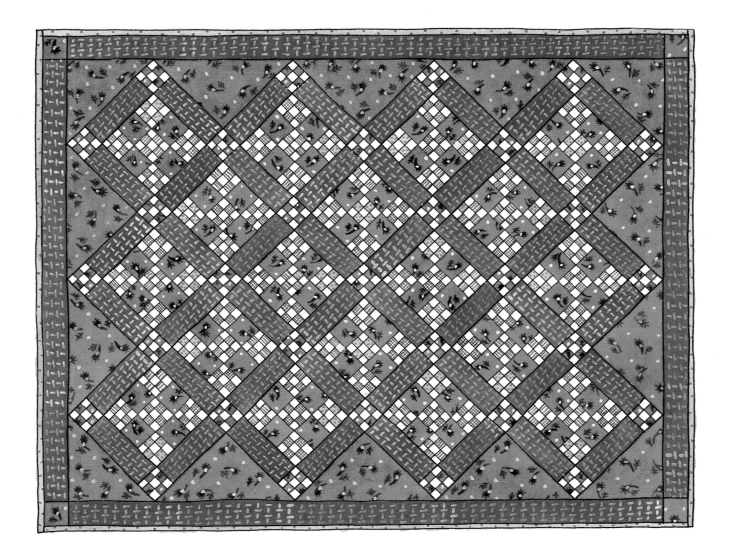

This quilt combines five nine-patch blocks together with four unpieced squares to form the Double Nine-patch design. Here, the blocks are set on point and sashing is used to divide them. For added interest, the nine-patch element has been incorporated into the sashing as pieced corner posts.

Skill level: Intermediate
Finished quilt: 61 x 78 in / 154.9 x 198.1 cm
Finished block: 9 x 9 in / 22.8 x 22.8 cm
Number of blocks: 18

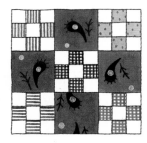

MATERIALS

Red print 2 yards / metres
Blue 2¹/2 yards / metres
White 1 yard / metre
Red scraps a total of ³/4 yard / metre
    (a piece 3¹/2 x 3¹/2 in / 8.9 x 8.9 cm will make
    one nine-patch block)
Wadding 65 x 82 in / 165.1 x 208.3 cm
Backing 4 yards / metres
Binding ¹/2 yard / metre

CUTTING INSTRUCTIONS

Blue fabric
1. Cut two strips, 3¹/2 x 81 in / 8.9 x 205.7 cm, and
two strips, 3¹/2 x 64 in / 8.9 x 162.6 cm for the
borders. Extra length has been allowed for
trimming to fit.
2. Cut 48 sashing strips, 3¹/2 x 9¹/2 in / 8.9 x 24.1 cm.

Red print fabric
1. Cut two squares, 18¹/4 x 18¹/4 in / 46.4 x 46.4 cm.
Cut across both diagonals to make four side
triangles.
2. Using one of these triangles as a template, cut
two more triangles with the straight grain running
along the longest side.
3. Cut two squares, 11¹/2 x 11¹/2 in / 29.2 x 29.2
cm diagonally in half to make four corner triangles.
4. For the plain squares in the double nine-patch
block, cut 72 squares, 3¹/2 x 3¹/2 in / 8.9 x 8.9 cm.

Cut four more squares of the same size for the
corner posts in the border.
5. For the nine-patch blocks which separate the
sashing strips, cut five strips, 1¹/2 / 3.8 cm wide
across the full width of the fabric.

White fabric
1. Cut 24 strips, 1¹/2 in / 3.8 cm long, across the
width of the fabric. Cut into 1¹/2 in / 3.8 cm
squares or leave in strips for quick-piecing.

Red scrap fabrics
1. Cut 360 squares, 1¹/2 x 1¹/2 in / 3.8 x 3.8 cm.

PIECING THE BLOCKS

1. For the scrap nine-patch blocks, first sew
squares into strips of three alternating colours, then
sew strips together. Piece 90 blocks altogether.
2. Sew a total of 18 double nine-patch blocks by
alternating pieced blocks with plain red print
squares.
3. Use the strip-piecing technique to make the 31
nine-patch blocks which form the corner posts in
the sashing strips. Sew red and white strips into
two sets: white / red / white, and red / white / red.
Press seam allowances towards the red strip.

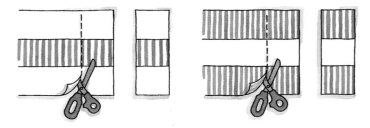

4. Cut the pieced strips apart at 1¹/2 in / 3.8 cm
intervals. You will need 31 red / white / red, and 62
white / red / white strips. Sew the strips together in
the correct order, taking care to match points.

orientation at the ends of the block rows, and sew on.

5. Sew sashing rows to block rows in the correct sequence.

6. Finally add corner triangles. Press the quilt thoroughly.

ADDING THE BORDERS

1. Pin, then sew the longer border strips to the top and bottom of the quilt. Press.

2. Sew corner posts to each end of the two remaining border strip. Press, then sew to the sides of the quilt.

PUTTING THE BLOCKS TOGETHER

Arrange blocks, sashing strips and pieced corner posts. Pin units together in diagonal rows, in the correct sequence. Press carefully after sewing each step.

1. Join corner nine-patch posts and sashing strips, noting number in each row.

2. Join blocks into rows separated by blue sashing strips, noting number of blocks in each row.

3. Sew a blue sashing strip at each end of the rows of blocks.

4. Position the side triangles in the proper

QUILTING AND FINISHING

1. Press the quilt top well on the back and front. Cut off any loose threads.

2. From the selection of quilting patterns, mark a design using your preferred method. Straight line quilting can be marked with 1/4 in / 6 mm tape as you work, or measured by eye.

3. Assemble the quilt layers, and baste in a grid.

4. Quilt, working from the centre out towards the border.

5. Finish with a straight binding as directed in the Techniques section.

MANDARIN CHEQUERBOARD

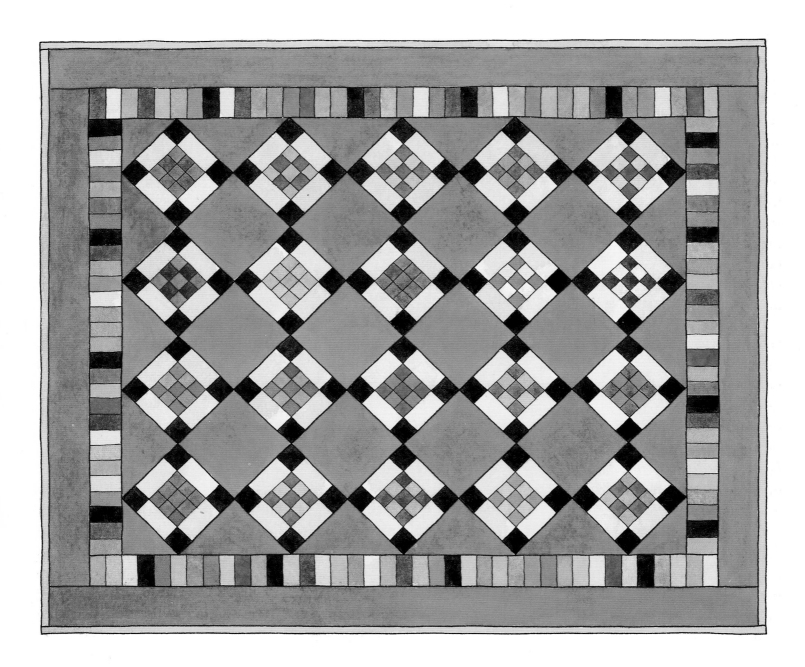

Elements of the first three quilts are combined in this final version;
a small nine-patch is set into the centre of the block, and pieced
blocks, on point alternate with plain coloured setting squares.

BASIC TECHNIQUES

Fabrics for Patchwork

The ideal fabric for quiltmaking is 100% dress-weight cotton. Many fabric manufacturers are now designing specifically for patchwork, and the selection of both solid and printed materials is enormous. A visit to a quilting supply store will demonstrate this. Many shops provide a mail order service, some boasting over 1,000 different fabrics from which to choose. If you are planning to use scrap fabrics left over from dressmaking or other projects, similar weights of fabric must be used next to each other. Combining heavy and light-weight fabrics together will lead to puckering and uneven wear.

When choosing fabrics for a quilt, remember that the success of many designs relies on the contrast between dark, medium and light values and their position within the block. This is particularly true of scrap quilts, many of which have a richness of texture afforded by the use of many different fabrics. The tonal values you use, that is the degree of dark and light, is as important as the colours you choose for your quilt.

All fabrics should be washed and ironed before use to preshrink and test for colour fastness. To prevent distortion, clip into the selvedge edges before washing. If any dye loss occurs, a solution of one part white vinegar to three parts cold water added to the rinsing water may help to fix it. Rinse until the water runs clear.

The amounts stated for the quilt projects are based on 45 in / 115 cm wide fabric and the yardage requirements given do not allow for errors in cutting out. If you are a beginner, it is advisable to add a little extra when buying fabric. Any left-over scraps can be used in future projects.

Templates

Templates must be accurate to ensure the success of a quilt. They are printed with a solid cutting line for machine-piecing and a broken sewing line for hand-piecing. Be sure that you trace off the correct size for your chosen method of sewing. Tape template plastic or tracing paper over the printed shapes and trace, using a hard pencil with a sharp point. Template plastic can be cut out with paper scissors. If you use card, transfer the shape and cut out carefully. Mark the grain lines onto the templates and identify with the name and size of the block. Store sets of templates in labelled envelopes to avoid confusion.

If you plan to hand-piece your blocks, the template will be the size of the finished piece. A line is traced around the template directly onto the wrong side of the fabric and $1/4$ in / 6 mm seam allowance is added as you cut out each piece. The marked line is your sewing line. The cutting line can be marked with a quilter's quarter - a ruler with $1/4$ in / 6 mm sides - or a $1/4$ in / 6 mm tracing wheel, but you will soon gain confidence and be able to add the seam allowance by eye. If you plan to machine-piece, the seam allowance is included on the template when you trace and cut on the solid line.

Marking and cutting the fabric

Cut off the selvedges of the fabric and straighten

the crosswise grain, which is the edge that runs across the width of the fabric from selvedge to selvedge. Any long borders or sashing strips should be cut out first, to avoid having to make joins later. If you are using the same fabric on the back of the quilt as in the pieced top, remember to set aside enough before you start cutting the pieces.

If you are using templates, mark round them on the wrong side of the fabric positioning them correctly for the grain lines. If any of the shapes are asymmetrical, e.g. rhomboid, remember to reverse them when necessary to avoid cutting the mirror image. To eliminate the fabric dragging as you mark, use a sheet of sandpaper underneath the area being traced or the template can be stuck firmly onto sandpaper to prevent it slipping. If you are using hand-piecing templates (i.e. those without seam allowances added), remember to leave enough space between pieces to allow for the addition of seam allowances as you cut. Templates for machine-piecing can be placed and marked edge to edge.

Rotary cutting

Many of the simple shapes in patchwork can be cut without templates using the rotary cutting technique. The basic rotary cutting equipment consists of three items: a self-healing cutting board, the rotary ruler and the cutter itself. The board and the ruler are both marked with a grid and the ruler has a square, non-bevelled edge to stop the blade from slipping across when in use. Never use a rotary cutter with a flat or bevelled ruler as this could be extremely dangerous. Different sizes of each item are available, but a good set to begin with is a board 17 x 23 in / 43.2 x 58.4 cm, a ruler

6 x 24 in / 15.2 x 61 cm and the larger diameter cutter. Although the small cutter is slightly cheaper and can be useful when cutting very small pieces, it is not economical to buy. The blade rotates twice as many times, being half the size, and therefore becomes blunt more quickly, and the extra control afforded by the larger size makes it more worthwhile for general use.

A certain amount of practise is required to learn how to use the cutter effectively but once mastered it can reduce the time spent cutting by more than half. The sharp circular blade on the cutter is protected by a safety guard: get into the habit of putting the guard on each time you put the cutter down and always cut away from your body. A new blade can cut through up to eight layers of fabric and should last well if taken care of. If it seems to be getting blunt, a drop of sewing machine oil rubbed over the surface can sometimes prolong its life. When the blade does need replacing, be careful to reassemble the cutter correctly.

Prepare the fabric for cutting by first straightening and squaring the crosswise grain (selvedge to selvedge across the width) as follows: fold the fabric in half with selvedges together, then fold again placing the second fold in line with the

selvedges. Smooth the layers together and press, then place the fabric on the board. Position the ruler on the fabric with one of the horizontal grid lines even with the double fold which should be at the front of the board. Slide the ruler to the edge of the fabric then hold it down firmly while you push the cutter along the edge of the ruler to make the first cut, straightening the edges. By creating a 90° angle in the fabric as you cut, aligning a horizontal line on the ruler with the folded edges and the vertical edge of the ruler on the edges to be cut, you will ensure that the strips of fabric will be perfectly straight.

After the edge has been straightened, fabric can be cut into strips, squares, rectangles and triangles by using either the grid on the board or on the ruler. To use the grid on the board, place the fabric in line with both horizontal and vertical grid lines and cut the required sizes by lining up the ruler with the measurements on the board. To use the grid on the ruler, line up the appropriate measurement line on the ruler with the cut edge of the fabric, trapping the strip to be cut under the ruler, and cut.

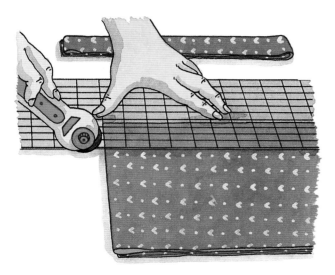

When using the grid on the ruler, the bulk of the fabric should be on the right if you are right-handed and on the left if you are left-handed.

Cut strips can be further cut into squares and rectangles. To cut half-square triangles, first cut squares then divide these across the diagonal from corner to corner.

PIECING THE BLOCKS

Making a sample block
Before cutting out the entire quilt, cut and piece together a sample block to check for accuracy and to make sure you are pleased with your fabric choices. Arrange the pieces on a flat surface in the correct position to determine the piecing sequence. The basic rule when sewing blocks is to sew smaller pieces together first into larger units of squares or rectangles according to the block design, join the resulting units into strips, then finally stitch these strips together.

Hand-piecing
Place the pieces right sides together and start the seam with a knot and a backstitch for extra security. Stitch the pieces together with a running stitch, along the pencil line beginning and ending at the seam allowance. At the end of the seam, finish with another backstitch and tidy the tail of the thread by weaving it in a few stitches before cutting.

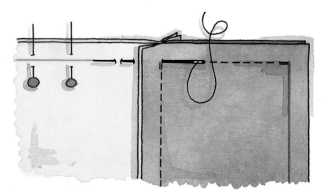

To cross a seam when joining rows together, take the needle through the seam allowance and continue sewing along the next patch so that seams remain free and can be pressed to whichever side will make the block flatter.

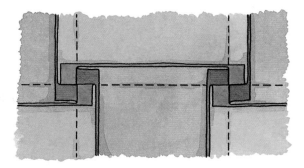

Wherever possible, seams should be spiralled to reduce bulk on the back of the block and pressed towards the darker fabric so that the seam allowance does not show through to the front.

There are many blocks which require a piece to be set into a corner angle created by two other pieces.

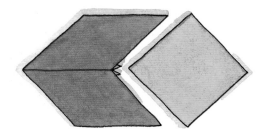

When the seam which creates the angle has been stitched, position the third piece along one edge of the angle and sew from the centre point to the edge, keeping within the seam allowance on the marked lines.

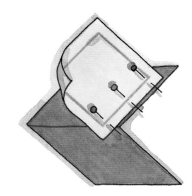

Pivot the patch through the angle and stitch along the second side again from the centre outward.

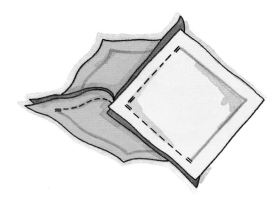

Steam press the seams away from the inset patch on the wrong side first, then on the right side for a smooth result.

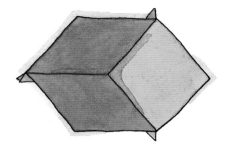

When joining pieces which meet at an angle other than a right angle, for example, diamonds and some triangles, offset the pieces so that the stitching lines, rather than the cut edges are aligned.

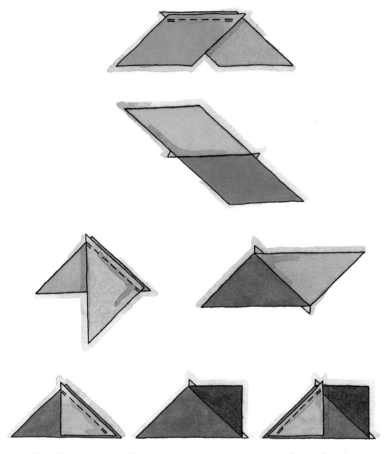

Whether you choose to machine-or hand-piece, make sure you have joined the pieces correctly before adding the next piece.

Machine-piecing

Pieces for machine-piecing have no marked sewing line and should be stitched from edge to edge.

Chain-piecing will speed up the process, i.e. feeding pairs of pieces through the machine without cutting the threads between them. Make sure raw edges are together and that you sew an accurate 1/4 in / 6 mm seam allowance. As you assemble the block, press all seams and match appropriate points by locking the seam allowances together in opposite directions.

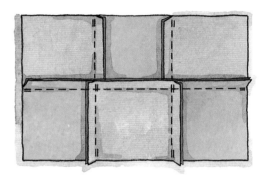

Most sewing machines can be adjusted to stitch 1/4 in / 6 mm from the raw edges, either with a special quilting foot or by adjusting the needle position. If this is not possible on your machine, mark the throat plate with several layers of masking tape in the correct position to build up a ridge along which fabric can be guided the correct distance from the raw edges.

Borders

Most of the quilts featured in this collection have simple borders which balance and contain the central designs. Handling a quilt top while work is in progress often stretches the edges, so it is more reliable to measure the length and width of the quilt across the centre from edge to edge for the final border measurements. All border measurements include a generous amount for trimming to fit.

With straight cut borders, such as those used in the Amish Bear's Paw quilt, measure and cut the first two border strips and attach to opposite sides. The remaining two border pieces must accommodate the additional width of the border pieces already attached.

Another border option is borders with corner posts, as in the Amish Nine-patch, Amish Diamond in a Square and several other quilts. Cut border pieces, two each for the length and width of the quilt. Cut squares for the corner posts to measure the same as the width of the borders. Join two border pieces to opposite sides of the central design. Press, then sew a corner post to each short side of the remaining two borders before sewing these to the quilt top, matching the seams at intersections.

Multiple borders, used very successfully in the Mennonite Log Cabin and Mennonite Irish Chain quilts, combine two or three border strips for an effective frame to the central design. Strips are first joined together to make a pieced border strip, then applied to the quilt as a single unit. Corners can be straight, mitred or finished with corner posts.

Mitred borders provide an elegant finish, but require at least 5 in / 12.7 cm excess at each end of the border pieces to accommodate the mitre.

To mitre a border:

a. Join the borders to the edges of the quilt, beginning and ending your seam ¹/4 in / 6 mm from the edges. Place the quilt top right side down on a

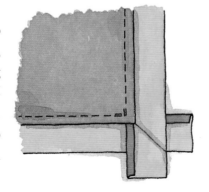

flat surface and fold one border over the other. Draw a straight line from the inner corner at a 45° angle to the border.

b. Reverse the position of the borders and repeat.

c. With the right sides of the border pieces together, stitch along the marked lines which should match up exactly, from the inner to the outer corner. In order to do this you will have to fold the quilt diagonally from the corner you are working on.

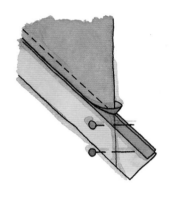

d. Before trimming away excess fabric open the corner seam and press to check that it lies flat.

Marking the quilting pattern

After the quilt top is pieced and borders attached, it must be marked with a quilting design. Simple straight line or contour quilting which outlines the pieced shapes can be stitched by eye or marked as you work with ¹/4 in / 6 mm masking tape. This method can be used after the three layers of the quilt have been assembled. Remove masking tape after each quilting session to avoid leaving a sticky residue. It is best to mark more complicated quilt designs before assembling the layers so you have a firmer surface to mark against. Marking through soft wadding may distort the design.

Quilting templates can be made by tracing the designs from the book and cutting them from card or template plastic. If required, enlarge quilting designs on a photocopier before preparing templates. For interior lines, cut channels with a craft knife.

Another way of transferring the quilting design is by tracing it directly onto the fabric. Place a full size drawing of the quilting pattern done in black marker pen underneath the fabric in the correct position and tape it down. The design should show through lighter fabrics but it may be necessary to use a light box if working with dark fabric. Make a temporary one by placing a light underneath a glass-topped table to try this method.

Ideally, the marking should be visible while you quilt and be easily removed afterwards. Possible choices are a hard lead pencil which is fine enough to be covered by the quilting stitches or an artist's coloured pencil, a water-soluble felt tip fabric marker, chalk pencil or tracing wheel and dressmakers' carbon paper, or even a sliver of white soap. Whatever you use, test it first on a piece of scrap fabric.

ASSEMBLING THE QUILT LAYERS

Trim off any loose threads on the back of the quilt and give it a final pressing. Pressing is not recommended after layering as this will compress

and may fuse the wadding. If necessary, prepare the backing by joining pieces of fabric. Remove the selvedges and press the seam to one side.

Working on a large flat surface, spread out the backing fabric wrong side up, then tape the corners down. Centre the wadding and the quilt top on the backing and smooth out the wrinkles, pulling gently from opposite ends. Use 2 oz wadding available in various fibres and sizes. Cut a piece to the specified size, if possible, as any joins in the wadding form a potentially weak area. If you cannot avoid a join, fasten the edges together with a herringbone stitch so that it is flat, and try to position the join under an area of close quilting.

The backing and wadding should be about 3 - 4 in / 7.6 - 10.2 cm larger than the quilt top on each side. When all three layers are smoothed together, baste them with large stitches working from the centre outwards to each corner, and then in a grid with the lines about 5 in / 12.7 cm apart.

If you plan to machine quilt, the three layers can be secured with safety pins every 4 - 6 in / 10.2 - 15.2 cm. Try to position them so they will not be in the way as you quilt.

QUILTING

Hand-quilting

Quilting stitches are small, even running stitches, which go through all three layers of the quilt, securing them together and adding a decorative texture to the quilt surface. The needle used for quilting is called a 'between'. Use size 8, 9 or 10 according to your preference.

Thread your needle with a length of quilting thread no longer than 18 in / 45.7 cm and knot the end. With your basted quilt held taut in a quilting hoop and working from the centre of the quilt towards the edges, insert the needle into the quilt top a small distance away from the point at which you plan to start. Tug the thread until the knot pops through and embeds itself in the wadding. Use a thimble on the middle finger of the sewing hand, keeping the other hand underneath the work to guide the needle back up. Many quilters also use a thimble with a flattened top on a finger of the guiding hand which helps to push up the needle and protects the finger. Take three or four stitches

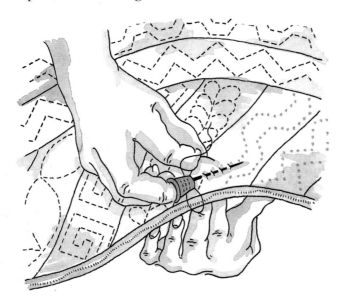

with a rocking movement, keeping the thumb pressed down on the fabric just ahead of the stitching. Try to keep stitches as even as possible - this is more important than size. When the thread becomes too short, tie a knot close to the quilt surface and pop it through to the inner layers.

Opinion varies as to which design of quilting hoop or frame is best, but the work should not be fastened in too tightly. Baste strips of fabric approximately 9 in / 22.8 cm wide down the sides of the quilt so that the hoop can be positioned correctly to quilt the outer edges. Remove these strips, and basting stitches when quilting is complete.

Machine-quilting

The continuous and regular line of machine-made stitches gives machine quilting a different quality from the softer texture of hand-quilting. If your machine has an even feed mechanism or a walking foot, this will make machine-quilting easier. Use a slightly longer stitch than you would for sewing seams and check that the tension is right for quilting on a sample piece - it may have to be loosened slightly. Keep the quilt rolled up tightly to make it easier to pull through the machine and work on a large table to support the weight. Flatten the area you are working on by holding your hands in a triangle with thumbs together. Safety pins may have to be repositioned as you work, or extra pins put into the area you are working on. Try to avoid any pleats forming on the back of the quilt; this is more likely to happen where quilting lines cross each other so check the back occasionally to prevent this.

Matching or contrasting thread can be used, or you could opt for invisible nylon thread. Available in either clear or grey for darker fabrics, the invisible thread is good for quilting 'in-the-ditch' where the quilting stitches are sunk into the seams between pieces. Thread the machine with nylon, but use ordinary cotton for the bobbin in a colour that matches the quilt backing. If you can, work from the centre of the quilt towards the outer edges and either begin and end each line with a few small backstitches, or pull threads through to the back of the quilt, knot them together and thread them into the middle layer. Where lines of quilting run off the edges, just trim the ends as the final binding will enclose and secure them. Continuous line patterns make for less untidy ends to finish off, so try and devise a machine-quilting pattern which utilises this technique.

BINDING AND FINISHING

Straight binding

Cut strips of binding fabric 2¹/₂ in / 6.4 cm wide on the lengthwise or crosswise grain of the fabric. If strips need to be joined, use a diagonal seam to avoid bulk. Cut two each for the length and width of the quilt top. Allow a little extra for tidying the corners on the third and fourth strip. Trim away excess backing and wadding level with the quilt top. Fold the binding strips in half lengthwise, wrong sides together. Pin the binding strips to the sides of the quilt, right sides together, all raw edges matching. Machine stitch through all layers taking ¹/₄ in / 6 mm seam allowance. Fold the binding to the back and slipstitch the folded edge down, just over the stitching line to conceal it. On the second

and third sides of the quilt tidy each end of the binding strips before applying them and continue hemming stitches along the corners.

Bias binding

Although you need more fabric to make bias binding, it is more versatile because it stretches and can accommodate curved corners. One square yard / metre will make approximately 15 yards / metres of 2¹/₂ in / 6.4 cm wide binding. From a square of fabric, fold one corner down to form a diagonal crease, then cut into two triangles along the foldline.

With right sides facing, stitch the two triangles together taking a ¹/₄ in / 6 mm seam allowance and press the seam open. Use a small stitch as you will be cutting across the seams.

On the wrong side of the fabric draw parallel lines the required width of the binding strips (2¹/₄ in / 6.4 cm for folded binding) along the bias edges.

With right sides together, pin and stitch the straight grain edges of the fabric, offsetting the ends of the seam by the width of the bias strip and matching

the drawn lines. Press seams open. Continuous strips of bias binding can now be cut from the resulting cylinder of fabric along the marked lines.

Fold the binding in half with the seams inside and press, being careful not to stretch it.

To mitre the corners of bias binding, apply binding to the right side of the quilt beginning in the centre of one side, matching all raw edges. Fold in 1 in / 2.5 cm of the binding at the start and continue sewing up to ¼ in / 6 mm from the first corner. At the corner, fold the binding up at a 90° angle and press the crease. Take two or three backstitches and break the threads. Fold the binding down against the previous crease to meet the adjacent edge of the

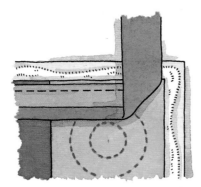

quilt. Stitch the binding to the next edge. Repeat for the other three corners.

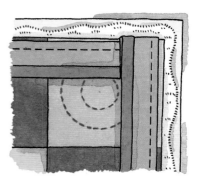

When the binding is attached all round the edges, join the two ends by overlapping the fold at the start. Fold the binding over to the back and slipstitch down. The crease will form a folded mitre on the front which can be left unstitched or fastened with a few small stitches.

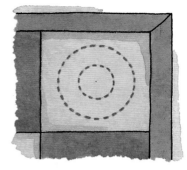

Self-binding

Centre the quilt top and wadding on the backing fabric so that an even border of backing projects beyond the edges of the quilt top and baste the layers together. When quilting is complete trim the wadding even with the quilt top. Cut away excess backing fabric to leave 1 in / 2.5 cm excess from the edges of the quilt top and wadding. Bring the backing over the quilt with a double fold, enclosing the raw edges. Pin or baste, then slipstitch down on the right side of the quilt. At the corners, fold the backing so that the point touches the corner point of the quilt top, and trim away excess fabric along the crease. Then fold the edges over to form a mitre and continue hemming round the corner.

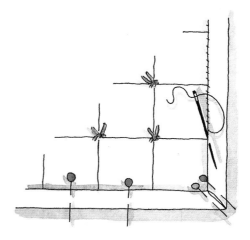

Fold-finishing
Trim away excess wadding ¼ in / 6 mm smaller than the raw edge of the quilt top. Trim excess backing away to leave ½ in / 1.3 cm. Fold the backing over to enclose the wadding. Fold the raw edge of the quilt top under and slipstitch the folds together.

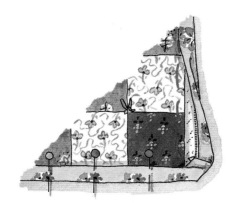

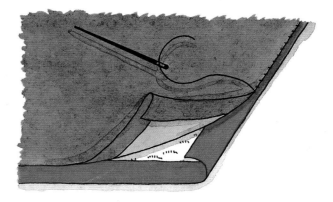

PIECING TEMPLATES

MENNONITE BOW-TIE

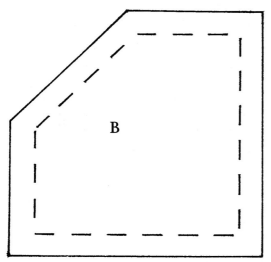

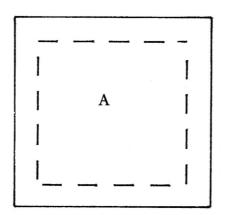

BASKETS

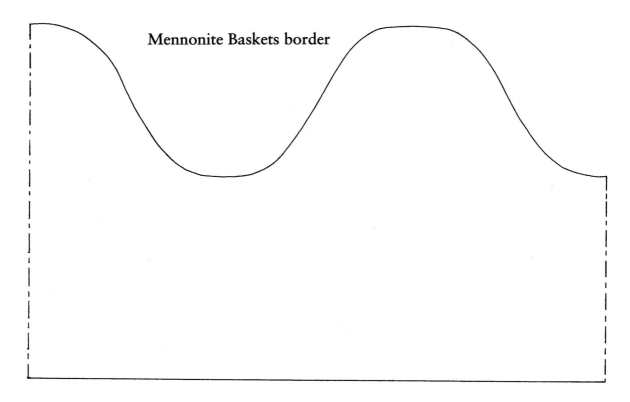

Mennonite Baskets border

QUILTING TEMPLATES

MENNONITE BOW-TIE

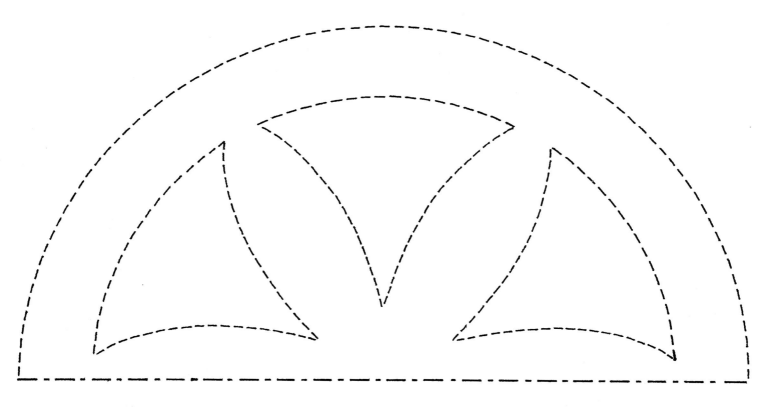

Bow-Tie ¹/₂ pattern

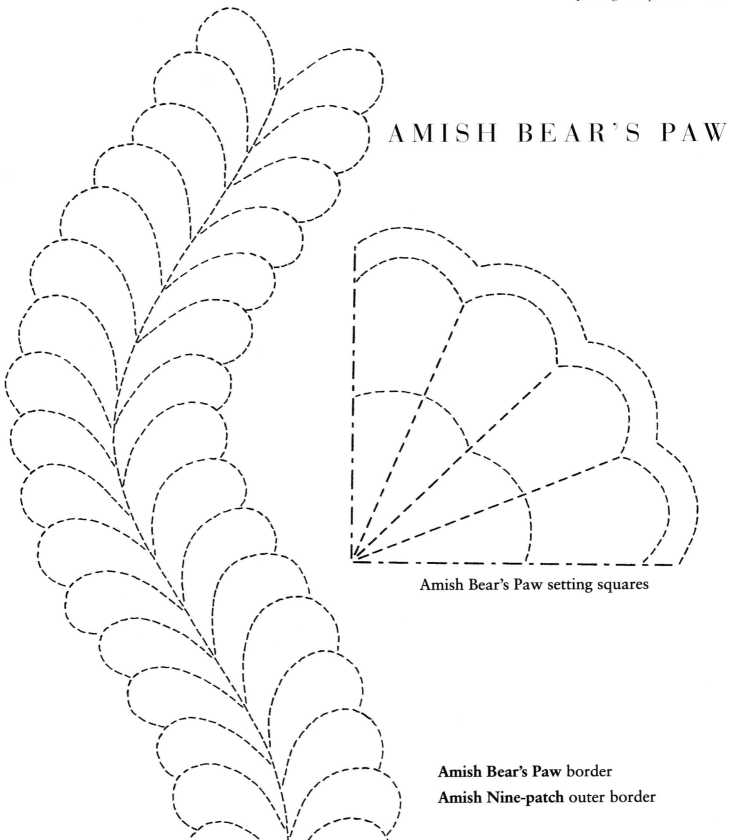

AMISH BEAR'S PAW

Amish Bear's Paw setting squares

Amish Bear's Paw border

Amish Nine-patch outer border

AMISH DIAMOND IN A SQUARE

Diamond in a Square border

Diamond in a Square enlarge 400%

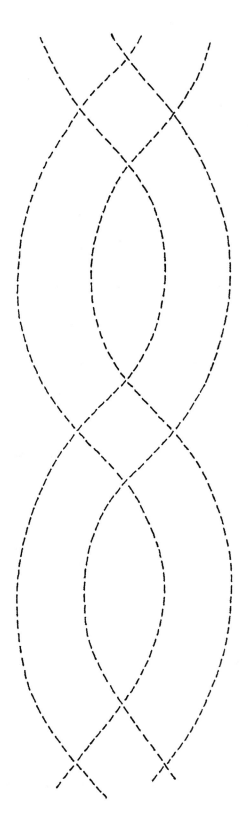

CABLE

Log Cabin Straight Furrows border

Double Irish Chain

Amish Nine-Patch

Joseph's Coat

B A R S

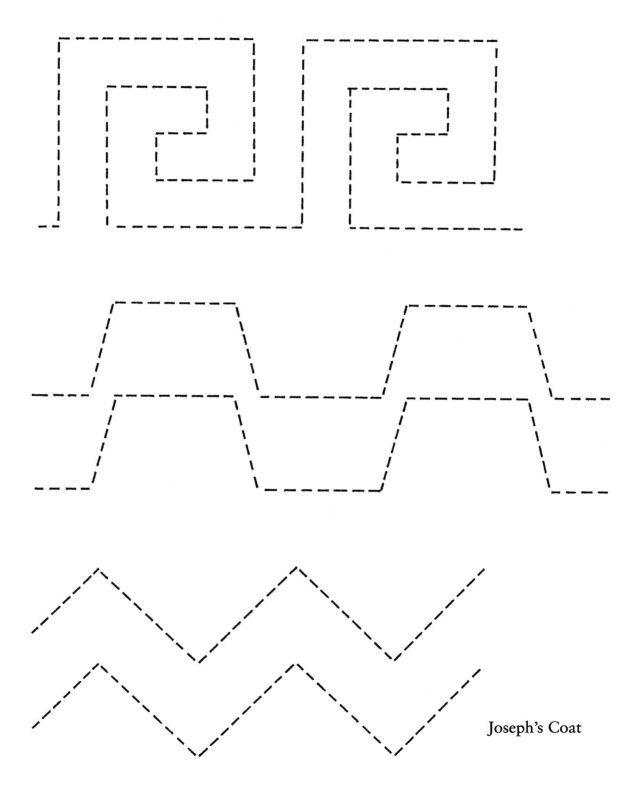

Joseph's Coat

Joseph's Coat